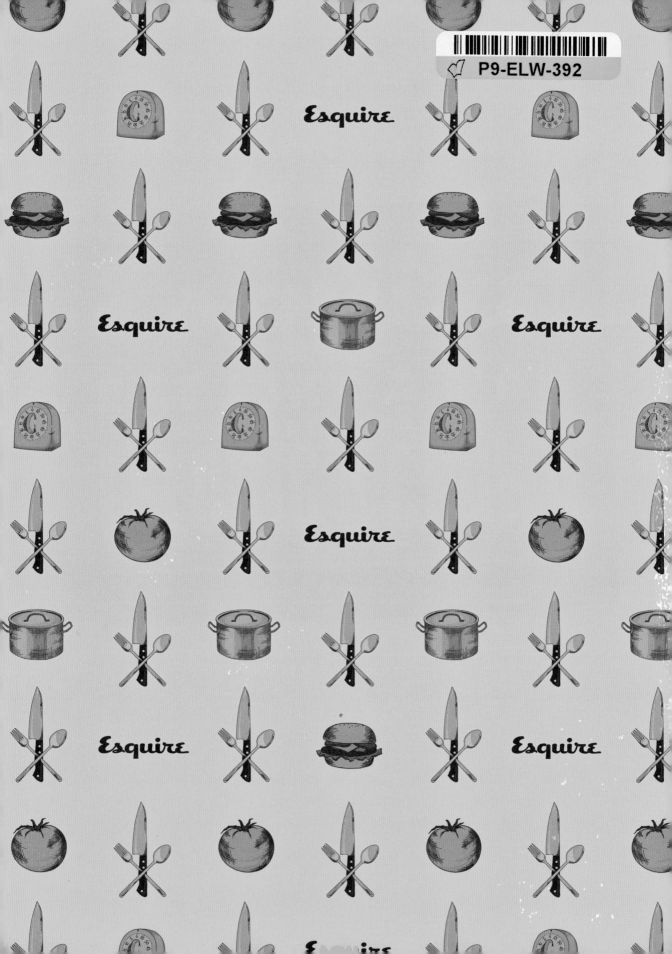

Esquire

The
EAT LIKE A MAN
GUIDE TO
FEEDING A CROWD

HOW TO COOK FOR FAMILY, FRIENDS, AND SPONTANEOUS PARTIES

Foreword by **BRYAN VOLTAGGIO**
Introduction by **DAVID GRANGER**

CHRONICLE BOOKS
SAN FRANCISCO

Page 224 constitutes a continuation of the copyright page.

Library of Congress Cataloging-in-Publication Data available.
ISBN 978-1-4521-3184-9

Manufactured in China

Designed by Erin Jang
Illustrations on pages 45, 47, 51, 66, 80, 127, 132, 178, 192,
and 214 by Amanda Sim

The information in this book has been carefully researched and
tested, and all efforts have been made to ensure accuracy. Neither
the publisher nor the creators can assume responsibility for any
accident, injuries, losses or other damages resulting from the use
of this book.

10 9 8 7 6 5 4 3 2 1

Chronicle Books LLC
680 Second Street
San Francisco, California 94107
www.chroniclebooks.com

Contents

Foreword

BRYAN VOLTAGGIO

PEOPLE DON'T LIKE to cook for me anymore. Somewhere along the way, my presence as a guest simply became a chore for the host, my RSVP an albatross. We do a dance where the hosts nervously ask if everything is okay, and I assure and comfort them profusely, saying, yes, indeed things are actually great; I even take a second helping as proof. I have a feeling they don't really believe me, but we usually leave it at that, moving on to another subject as the common courtesies have all been met. But still, I know, they wonder.

What they don't realize is that things are perfect. This is where the restaurant started: at the home table. Here lie the raw materials, the source of it all—the egg to the chicken.

I've experienced all the stages of chef-dom, from student cook exclusively devoted to all things culinary to chef leading brigades of compatriots through the battle of Saturday night service to a competitive television personality; but it was becoming a restaurateur that taught me that cooking, truly good cooking, is about generosity more than perfection. Polish all the silver and starch as many aprons as you want—if that emotional bond isn't there, tying the flavor to the experience, all of the technique in the world won't conjure up hospitality.

Pimento cheese on a Ritz can be as delicious as truffle mushroom bisque served in a delicate bone-china demitasse when served with the right sentiment. The more critically creative parts of my job, the parts that include liquid nitrogen, dehydrators, anti-griddles, ovens that I can program from my phone, and forceps that allow me to plate the most delicate of ingredient perfectly every time are just a small part of my job as a professional chef.

These sophistications have become the standard accoutrements of haute cuisine; but let me tell you, after all is said and done and strained twice through the chinoise, what you are left with is the essence of it all: Inspired cooking. I am a husband, a father, a son, and a neighbor, and I am inspired to cook every time and for whomever the "customer" may be, whether it's a late-night leftover meatball sandwich for a friend crashing over or chicken fingers for my kids. All it takes to be a good cook is an egg, a hungry person, and the desire to put a smile on their face.

Cooking for a group at home is a luxury for me these days, something covetable and elusive, akin to a relaxing hobby. With so many expectant mouths to feed in the community, cooking for guests outside of one of my restaurants or public functions is a downright enviable situation. When I do get the chance, I revel in the task; this is my mental yoga. Preparing a meal for guests at home removes the business from the chef-customer equation and allows me to disconnect from "the service," sip a beer while I work, plan the meal, and look forward to sitting down at a table with friends (something that never happens while I'm in my whites). I can become a civilian again, be a part of the conversation that exists outside the bounds of the food itself, and experience the meal from start to finish. The only thing I end up missing is my Olympic team of dishwashers.

Now it's your turn. If I were standing next to you in the kitchen, here is what I would tell you: Cooking for a group is tactical.

- **Plan something** you know, and practice a time or two with smaller batches.
- **Do what you can do** the day before, even peeling onions or carrots and washing bunches of herbs.
- **Get a big heavy-duty bag** and close an edge into a drawer just under the countertop near to where you will be working. The opening will sag down and create a big gaping maw that you can easily chuck things into as you go. (Most home garbage containers are too small for this kind of work.) Fill it up once and take it out before the guests arrive.
- **Have a nice big, heavy cutting board** as headquarters of operations, not one of those small plastic jobbies that is only suited for cutting bar fruit.
- **If people are arriving** at eight o'clock, plan to be done at seven o'clock.
- **People are going to want** to arrive and help. Set some tasks aside specifically for this; "dishes" is always a good answer if only to get them out of your hair for a minute.
- **If people insist** on bringing something, be specific about it. Leaving that kind of decision up to the guest means you can end up with three different 3-bean salads, all with the same three beans.
- **It's easier to make** one nice platter look better than assembling ten plates.
- **Let someone** else bring dessert.

Introduction

DAVID GRANGER | EDITOR IN CHIEF, *ESQUIRE*

NLIKE BRYAN VOLTAGGIO (see Foreword), I am not a good cook. I'm a fine amateur sous chef, meaning that I am competent at a lot of the tasks that aid my wife in creating a dinner party. But I'm just not a very good cook. I don't have the patience or the interest to spend a day (and sometimes more) making a meal.

And, yet, on occasion, I have enjoyed being the human responsible for feeding a significant number of people. I remember the first time I made a rendition of huevos rancheros for a bunch of friends and relatives who had spent the night. I'm not sure I had ever made them before. (If I had, it was just for myself.) I just decided to do it for, like, twelve. I knew how to fry up tortillas. I could imagine making a salsa-flavored black bean mash. I have made guacamole for my entire life. I can grate cheeses. I am capable of chopping tomatoes and lettuce and scallions. I had some good bottled salsa verde. I remembered that my favorite meal from my childhood was scrambled eggs cooked by my mom on a Coleman stove at the beach and that she first fried up breakfast sausage, crumbled it, and then poured the eggs into that very same pan and cooked 'em up. Thirty-five years later, I could still taste those sausage scrambled eggs.

So that's what I did: I made all those individual things, made coffee, put out juice, set the big round table on our deck, and then loaded all the component parts into bowls and onto warmed platters (where appropriate) and asked everyone to sit down and encouraged them to assemble their breakfasts. I can't say it was easy (it was work!) but it was uncomplicated—anyone with the will could have done it. And it was perfect. Of course, the perfection probably had as much to do with sitting outside, with a view of the river on a warm, sunny late morning, as it did with anything I had done. But, as with everything, it's all context.

We conversed, we basked, we ate until all the food was gone. People liked it. I felt like I'd accomplished something. I took a swim and a nap.

These are the times we live for—unforced camaraderie with people we like. And food, like drink, is the prop that makes it work. You can't just sit around looking at each other. Well, I suppose you can but that's a group therapy session. There's a reason holidays revolve around a big meal. You're gonna have a lot of people around. A group needs a raison d'être. The meal centers everyone, gives them a focus. For the entire day, you're either waiting for the meal, eating the meal, or recovering from the meal. And conversation and conviviality flow from that shared purpose.

The number of times we will spend with people we love, for no purpose beyond enjoying each other's company, is not infinite. I think we need all the encouragement we can get to create moments of simple enjoyment, pure relaxation. If this book does any single thing, I hope it will make it easier for you to enable those magical moments when a group of people enjoys each other. A get-together needs a meal—or at least a substantial snack. Nothing in this cookbook is hard. Every recipe is tested by both professionals as well as the amateurs at *Esquire* who love to eat with friends.

Go ahead. It'll be fun.

A Rallying Cry

MARIO BATALI

**IME WAS, YOU** were pretty sure that the best food was the kind that was the easiest to find. Or the kind you consume at a stadium, with a game going on in front of you. This was before everyone watched the Food Network and *Top Chef* and the sadistic reality shows hosted by that angry British chef who screams at his "cheftestants" until the veins in his neck bulge and his shrinking victims either cry or go to the hospital with heart trouble.

Well, my friend, the game has changed.

Cooking at home is now fully documented as cool, exceedingly good for you, fun to do, and, most significantly, an attractor of women. Plus, forces are conspiring to make it increasingly easy to do. When I was getting started, the books were a lot heavier, the guidance was much harder to find, and there wasn't a kitchen store (or two) in every mall. Like golf-club manufacturers, the kitchen-equipment folks constantly improve the tools of the trade, making nearly foolproof pots, pans, knives, steamers, pizza ovens, pasta rollers, and blenders, all virtually maintenance-free and priced to move. (You don't need a lot of gadgets, but if you want to indulge the male tendency to overstock the toolbox, you can.) And all the information you could want is constantly streaming at you like a runaway truck—books, newspaper stories, websites, apps, how-to videos, this essay I'm writing, even entire magazines devoted to single subjects like charcuterie or wedding cakes or pickles, all to help you source it, buy it, rub it, season it, roast it, braise it, frost it, sear it, stir-fry it, or, perhaps, *sous vide* it. You have power. I hope you'll use it. Like I said, you don't need much to get started.

Despite what most cookbooks and the Internet suggest, you really need only **THREE KNIVES**. I suggest an 8-in/20-cm chef's knife, a 4-in/10-cm paring knife, and a serrated bread knife. Buy another only when you know exactly why you need it. Opt for a national brand with forged-steel blades and a full tang, which sounds sexy but simply means the forged metal is a single piece running from the tip of the blade all the way through to the base of the handle.

Twelve-piece cookware sets for a "low, low price" are routinely hawked on late-night TV—often by friends of mine. But with a mere **FIVE PIECES**, you can do whatever you like—slay the dragon and then cook its tenderloin in the style of the Duke of Wellington, if you want to. I like cast iron coated with enamel for longevity as well as forgiveness if I happen to take my eyes off the prize while pouring Chianti. One 12-in/30.5-cm sauté pan, one 8-in/20-cm omelet pan, a 7- or 8-qt/7- or 8-L spaghetti pot with an insert, a roasting pan, and a 4-qt/4-L saucepan. That's it. When you are ready to tackle Moroccan cooking, I will help you find the *couscoussier*.

Now get a couple of basic **COOKBOOKS** with some nice pictures of things you want to eat. (There's one called *Eat Like a Man*, by *Esquire*. There are several by me. You could start with those.) Read through them, choose a few recipes you think you can handle, and follow the steps all the way to the eating part.

With that you can make virtually anything I can in about the same amount of time. Shop often, shop hard, and spend for the best stuff available—logic dictates that you can make delicious food only with delicious ingredients. There are two activities in life in which we can lovingly and carefully put something inside of someone we love. Cooking is the one we can do three times a day for the rest of our lives, without pills. In both activities, practice makes perfect.

EDWARD LEE | 610 MAGNOLIA | *Louisville, Kentucky*

Waffles and Eggs with Chicken Sausage and Green Chile Gravy

This is reinvented chicken and waffles—a classic Southern soul-food dish that has been a favorite of mine ever since I moved to Louisville. It's not an early-morning dish, but it is perfect for that not-quite-lunchtime meal when maybe you've had one too many bourbon cocktails the night before (my initial inspiration). The original version involves fried chicken dumped on top of waffles—a little extreme for a first meal of the day. I wanted to bring the dish full circle back to an identifiable breakfast (hence the eggs), but it had to retain its Southern roots (hence the gravy). Finally, I adore a little spice in the morning to wake up the spirit, but not so much as to ruin the rest of my day. Green chiles in a can are the perfect moderate choice, especially when your previous evening wasn't so moderate. Just be sure to make a few extra waffles— in my experience, there's always one person who hogs them all.

SERVES

16

LEVEL of DIFFICULTY

WORTH THE EFFORT

REASONABLE

EASY

4 tsp peanut oil or corn oil

2 lb/910 g raw chicken sausage (seasoned simply), removed from casings and crumbled

6 oz/170 g thick slab bacon, finely diced

1 yellow onion, diced

4 garlic cloves, minced

½ cup/60 g all-purpose flour

3 cups/720 ml milk

1 ¼ cups/300 ml buttermilk

Four 4-oz/113-g cans chopped green chiles

3 tsp coarse salt

2 tsp freshly ground black pepper

1 tsp paprika

16 large eggs

16 home-style waffles (your favorite homemade, or even store-bought frozen and defrosted ones are fine)*

½ cup/110 g unsalted butter, melted

1 small bag pork rinds

1 bunch scallions, green parts only, coarsely chopped →

* *Frozen waffles should be defrosted first or they will steam instead of crisping.*

1. Position one rack in the middle and one rack in the lower third of the oven and preheat to 375°F/190°C. Find two deep, ovenproof skillets that are about 12 in/30.5 cm wide. Make sure neither has a plastic handle that will melt in the oven. (If it does, throw it away and buy yourself a better skillet.)

2. Heat 2 tsp of the oil in each skillet over high heat until very hot. Add half of the sausage and half of the bacon to each and lower the heat to medium. Cook, stirring and breaking up any clumps with a spoon, until the meats are nicely browned, 5 to 7 minutes. Add half the onion and garlic to each skillet and cook, stirring, until the aromatics begin to brown, 3 to 5 minutes. Lower the heat a little more. Working with one skillet at a time, sprinkle in ¼ cup/30 g of the flour, stirring constantly, to make a quick roux. Keep stirring until the sausage is well coated and the flour has absorbed the pan fat, 2 to 3 minutes. (Watch the roux with an eagle eye, as it will burn quickly. As soon as the mixture turns a light amber color, immediately take it off the heat and keep stirring, because the hot pan will continue to cook the roux.)

3. When you're done cooking the roux in both pans, return them to medium-low heat. To each skillet, add 1½ cups/360 ml milk, ½ cup/120 ml buttermilk, half of the chiles, 1½ tsp salt, 1 tsp pepper, and ½ tsp paprika. Stir constantly until the gravy flows from your spoon in a steady stream, not clumps, about 8 minutes. (The gravy will look sort of shiny when the flour is cooked out.)

4. Turn off the heat and crack 8 eggs over the surface of the gravy in each skillet. (Crack the eggs close to the surface to keep the yolks intact.) Drizzle 2 tbsp buttermilk evenly over the surface of the eggs in each pan. Transfer both skillets to the middle rack in the oven.

5. Working quickly, arrange the waffles on a baking sheet and drizzle the melted butter over them. Slip the waffles onto the lower rack and bake along with the eggs. The eggs are done when the whites turn opaque and the yolks are set but still runny inside, 12 to 18 minutes. (Keep a good watch, as the yolks can quickly overcook. The cooking time for your eggs will vary depending upon your oven.) The waffles should be perfectly toasted at the same time the eggs are ready.

6. Cut the waffles on the diagonal to make four small triangles out of each and pile them on a platter. As a last bit of culinary genius, grab the pork rinds and crush them right in the bag until evenly crumbled. Sprinkle this right over the eggs, along with the chopped scallions and a little salt and coarsely ground pepper.

7. To serve, put the hot skillets on a folded kitchen towel or trivets in the center of the table, with a serving spoon and the waffle points alongside. Tell your eaters to take a waffle point or three and scoop an egg and lots of the gravy on top.

JOHN FITZSIMONS | **U.S. MILITARY ACADEMY** | *West Point, New York*

West Point Pancakes

The secret to the pancake recipe used at West Point is the combination of cake flour for maximum fluff and bread flour for an extra boost of protein. It's so good, you may want to make the full 8,000-pancake batch, which takes 1,440 eggs and 390 pounds of flour. Or try this.

SERVES

6

LEVEL *of* **DIFFICULTY**

WORTH THE EFFORT

REASONABLE

EASY

WET INGREDIENTS
2 cups/480 ml buttermilk
1½ cups/360 ml whole milk
4 large eggs
2 tbsp vanilla extract

DRY INGREDIENTS
5 cups/635 g cake flour
¾ cup/90 g bread flour
½ cup/100 g sugar
2 tbsp baking powder

¼ cup/55 g butter, melted
Vegetable oil for cooking

1. Measure all the Wet Ingredients into a bowl and mix with a fork or a hand mixer until the mixture is all one color.

2. Measure all the Dry Ingredients into a separate bowl. Mix well with a fork.

3. Slowly add the dry ingredients to the wet. Mix gently with a fork, scraping down the sides of the bowl. Leave some lumps.

4. Mix in the butter thoroughly.

5. Heat a large, nonstick skillet or flat griddle over medium-high heat. When the pan is really hot—a drop of water should sizzle immediately on contact—oil lightly with vegetable oil. Ladle out about ⅓-cup/75-ml portions of the batter, and spread out the batter. Cook until the bottoms are golden brown and the bubbles on top burst, then flip and cook on the other side for about 2 minutes.

6. Serve hot off the griddle and ladle on the next batch.

How to Feed an Actual Army

TYLER CABOT

Pancakes for four thousand in the West Point mess hall?
It's like anything—just break it down into its simplest parts.

It's the type of tub you could lose a small child in. Waist-deep, wide as a hockey goal, and filled with pancake batter. There are two of them, 60 gallons each. The evening before, after the dinner shift, two men filled them up: 31½ gallons of whole milk, 24 gallons of buttermilk, 180 pounds of eggs. Forty-two pounds of sugar, 390 pounds of flour, 6 gallons of shortening. And don't forget the salt—2¼ pounds of salt. And 6 gallons of vanilla extract. It's

just after midnight now in the kitchen at West Point. A man named Wally, gray hair tucked under his white paper cook's cap, adds 30 pounds of baking powder—it must go in closer to cooking time or the batter will ferment. He is methodical and trustworthy—been working this job for thirty-four years. He finishes at 2:30 A.M., four and a half hours before more than four thousand cadets will converge in the mess hall for breakfast. They'll come all at once, and they'll eat all at once. In under ten minutes. Wally has a lot of pancakes to cook.

The kitchen extends beyond view in every direction, an industrial-steel landscape that could be the set of a gory horror film—deep fryers the size of minivans, dunk tanks of boiling water, mixers with paddles you could canoe with. John Fitzsimons, the food-service officer, watches over his team of sixteen cooks. He has worked at West Point for twenty-four years, sets the menu, orders all the food. He wears loose-fitting khakis, button-down shirts that balloon, and scuffed black leather shoes. He's laconic, has a habit of looking down, as if always in private thought. "Just simple," he says, explaining how he feeds the masses. "We try to break it down to the simplest level."

There are advantages to feeding the U.S. Army. John knows exactly how many pancakes the cadets will eat. He knows how much butter, fat, and salt to use—Army calorie regulations. (All recipes are approved by a staff dietician.) There are no surprises, no uninvited guests. Just a task: Cook eight thousand pancakes in three hours. Just simple: Those 60-gallon tubs of batter are divided into 30-gallon bowls that are placed near the grills. The cooks then dunk and fill 1-gallon pitchers, off-loading the batter into the ½-gallon pitchers they use to hand-pour each pancake, carefully laying them out in grids of forty-eight. Wally works methodically, left to right, first pouring a batch, then starting over at the beginning to flip. To serve by seven o'clock, Wally must flip three hundred pancakes per hour.

4:45 A.M.

As they come off the flattop, the pancakes are placed on serving dishes, fifteen per, then rushed over to the forty-eight double-oven-size warmers on the far end of the room. Each warmer has slots for ten trays of food, enough to feed ten tables of ten cadets. And each warmer has a numbered spot in the mess hall, so once the cadets arrive, the waiters will have to walk only a few feet to serve each table.

There is no yelling—no talking really. Just flipping and carrying. Clangs as trays slide into warmers, and metallic buckles as warmer doors are swung shut. Most of the

cooks have been on the job for five, ten, even twenty years. Most wear pink earplugs.

5:30 A.M.

Darren, tasked today with loading the warming carts, tells John they're full. Instantly, John calls it: Stop grilling. Spatulas down. The little remaining batter is wheeled away. Scrapers and huge hoses come out, and in twenty minutes the griddles and workspace are clean, the residue of eight thousand pancakes wiped away and washed down the drain.

6:00 A.M.

The waiters take over. They spill into the room, about two football fields wrapped in wood and stone walls lined with oil portraits of military figures draped in state and Revolutionary flags, and crowned with stained-glass windows that depict giant battles. There are 6 wings in all, each filled with tables of 10 for 465 in total, meticulously set with plates, glasses, coffee cups, silverware, and bottles of every condiment imaginable—

syrup, ketchup, hot sauce, peanut butter, salad dressing, sugar. Having everything ready and at hand is key to the ten-minute breakfast.

6:57 A.M.

In they trickle, wearing boots, camo pants, and black fleece jackets. Many yawn, some carry notebooks. This is the same drill, the same mandatory breakfast every weekday. Underclassmen gather yogurt, milk, fruit, and Gatorade bars for the table from plastic rolling bins the size of playpens while upperclassmen wait bleary-eyed behind their chairs and the waiters stand ready at their assigned warming carts.

7:00 A.M.

It comes, loud and gruff and on time, as it has for decades:

"Attention. *Take seats!*"

There is no rush. No running. No fighting over syrup or silverware. The warmer doors swing open and, in seconds, the trays of pancakes and sausage emerge, warm and ready. The cadets eat determinedly, quietly, chewing slowly. Some pass on the pancakes in favor of cereal. One upperclassman passes on everything—he's facedown on the table asleep. But it's all orderly. Controlled and methodical chaos. About ten minutes after the cadets take their seats, most of the trays are empty, some sausage lingering, and the voice booms once more: "Cadets *rest!*"

And they are gone.

Johnnycakes

There's no mistaking the sweet, pebbly punch of cornmeal. Just don't tell a Rhode Islander that you're making johnnycakes with anything other than the state's signature white cornmeal, ground by a process that leaves the particles flat rather than granular. This recipe comes from Kenyon's Grist Mill (kenyons gristmill.com) in Usquepaug, where they've been grinding it properly since 1886. The cakes are lighter and lacier than your typical flapjack, with a slightly crunchy crust that holds up nicely under a slathering of jam or a puddle of warm maple syrup.

SERVES

4

(makes about 24 silver-dollar-size cakes)

LEVEL of DIFFICULTY

WORTH THE EFFORT

REASONABLE

EASY

1 cup/140 g finely ground white cornmeal
1 tsp sugar
½ tsp salt
1¼ cups/300 ml boiling water
Bacon fat or unsalted butter for greasing the griddle
Warm maple syrup for serving

1. Heat a well-seasoned griddle over medium-high heat, or preheat an electric griddle to 380°F/193°C.

2. Combine the cornmeal, sugar, and salt in a heatproof mixing bowl with high sides. Gradually add the boiling water, stirring until the mixture is smooth and thick enough to plop off the spoon. (The goal is to scald the cornmeal with the boiling water, which essentially cooks it in the bowl.) Stir using the back of the spoon—smooth-side up, concave-side down—to eliminate splatters while you pour.

3. Test your griddle to make sure it's the right medium-hot: a drop of water should skitter on the cooking surface. Grease it well with bacon fat. Drop the batter by table-spoonsful onto the griddle. Using the edge of the spoon, chop across the surface of the batter to release air. Let the johnnycakes sit until the edges begin to brown, about 6 minutes, then flip them and keep frying until the cakes are cooked through, about 6 minutes longer.

4. Transfer to warmed serving plates and serve hot with maple syrup.

TIP

This recipe can easily be doubled or tripled. Keep the finished johnnycakes warm in a low (200°F/95°C) oven while you fry up all the batter.

LEE BAILEY | ADAPTED BY THE *ESQUIRE* KITCHEN | *New York, New York*

Corn Fritters

Doughnuts, beignets, *zeppole,* sopapillas—almost every cuisine has a fried-batter breakfast food, and in the American South they're called *fritters*. Originally concocted by Afro-Caribbean slaves using American ingredients, this adaptation comes from the late Southern food writer Lee Bailey, who made two suggestions: The batter should be just thick enough that you must use a second spoon to urge it off the first, and your fritters must be small enough to cook all the way through without burning the exterior.

SERVES

6

(makes about 24 fritters)

LEVEL *of* **DIFFICULTY**

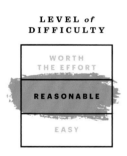

WORTH THE EFFORT

REASONABLE

EASY

Peanut oil for frying
1 cup/140 g white cornmeal
⅓ cup/40 g all-purpose flour
2 tsp baking powder
¾ tsp salt
2 large eggs, lightly beaten
1 cup/240 ml creamed corn
4 to 6 tbsp/60 ml to 90 ml milk
Warm maple syrup for serving

1. Preheat the oven to 200°F/95°C.

2. Pour oil into a heavy saucepan to a depth of at least 3 in/7.5 cm but no more than halfway up the sides. Heat the oil over medium-high heat to 365° to 375°F/185° to 190°C. (A long-stemmed deep-frying thermometer is ideal here. If you don't have one, just heat the oil until the surface shimmers and a drop of batter browns on contact.)

3. In a large bowl, whisk together the cornmeal, flour, baking powder, and salt. In a small bowl, stir together the eggs and creamed corn, then mix into the dry ingredients. Stir in the milk, 2 to 3 tbsp at a time, until the batter is workable but quite thick (see recipe introduction).

4. Working in small batches, drop the batter by the spoonful into the hot oil and cook until lightly browned, 3 to 4 minutes. Using a slotted spoon, transfer the fritters to paper towels to drain. Keep warm in the oven while you make the rest of the fritters, adjusting the heat under the oil as needed to maintain a fairly consistent temperature. Transfer the fritters to warmed serving plates and serve with maple syrup.

Hangtown Fry

Popularized in the late 1800s by gold prospectors in Hangtown (which is in El Dorado County, California, and was originally named for the frequency of hangings that occurred there until it was renamed Placerville in 1854), this meal was a one-dish mixture of the most expensive ingredients new money could buy: oysters transported from the San Francisco Bay in barrels, bacon, and eggs. It's still an extravagance of flavor, the luxurious richness of the eggs enhanced by the meaty, salty oysters and smoky bacon.

These simple, stunning omelets are perfect for a houseful of guests waking up at various times, with you manning the stove.

SERVES

LEVEL *of* DIFFICULTY

WORTH THE EFFORT

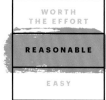

REASONABLE

EASY

2 cups/280 g yellow cornmeal
2 cups/255 g all-purpose flour
Coarse salt and freshly ground black pepper
Peanut oil for frying
20 oysters, shucked and drained (see page 37) or high-quality jarred
20 thick strips bacon
20 large eggs

1. In a large, shallow bowl, whisk together the cornmeal, flour, 2 tsp salt, and 1 tbsp pepper.

2. Pour the oil into a small, heavy saucepan to a depth of at least 3 in/ 7.5 cm but no more than halfway up the sides. Heat the oil over medium-high heat to 375°F/190°C. Dredge the oysters in the cornmeal mixture until well coated. Working in batches and using tongs, gently lower the oysters into the hot oil and fry, stirring once or twice, until crisp and golden, about 2 minutes. Using the tongs or a slotted spoon or skimmer, transfer to paper towels to drain, then place on a baking sheet in a low (200°F/93°C) oven to keep warm.

3. In a large skillet over medium-high heat, cook the bacon until crisp. Transfer to paper towels to drain, then crumble. Reserve the drippings in the pan.

4. For each omelet, in a 7-in/17-cm nonstick omelet pan or skillet, heat about 1 tbsp of the bacon drippings. In a small bowl, lightly beat 2 eggs, and season with salt and pepper. Add the eggs to the pan and stir until the eggs begin to thicken, about 1 minute. Add a small handful of the crumbled bacon and gently shake the pan back and forth to loosen the edges. Cook until the center of the omelet is set, 1 to 2 minutes. Tilt the skillet over a warmed plate and let the eggs roll out, flipping them over into an oval shape. Top with 2 fried oysters. Repeat until everyone has been served.

SERVES

1

(multiply for as many as you are willing to make)

LEVEL *of* **DIFFICULTY**

WORTH THE EFFORT

REASONABLE

EASY

Breakfast Burritos

For me, cooking at home is less about being a chef and more about being a dad. I have a limited time frame and a "do no harm" attitude in the kitchen; I don't want to burden myself with a lot of cleanup. This breakfast works on all counts, including the most important consideration: My kids will eat it. The flexibility is another bonus. Because children's tastes change quickly, I can get them to experiment with flavors by doing something as simple as switching out the salsa—we've gone through tomato, mango, and peach. Although adding avocado might work in some houses, it doesn't fly in mine. Right now, the eggs are scrambled with bacon, and sometimes I use breakfast sausage. I'm working them up to chorizo.

2 to 3 thick slices bacon (more sweet than smoky, such as maple-and-black-pepper cured or applewood smoked), cut into ½-in/12-mm dice

EASY SPICED BLACK BEANS*
One 15-oz/425-g can good-quality black beans in their liquid (do not drain)
Pinch of ground cumin
Pinch of chili powder
½ tsp salt, or to taste (the amount will vary according to the brand of your beans)

2 tbsp cold black coffee
1 tbsp rendered bacon fat

2 large eggs, lightly beaten with 1 tsp half-and-half
2 tbsp shredded mild cheese, such as a mix of Monterey Jack and Cheddar
One 10-in/25-cm flour tortilla
Pico de gallo, drained, for serving

1. Put the bacon in a small skillet over medium heat and cook slowly until the fat has liquefied but the bacon is still soft, about 8 minutes. Leaving the bacon in the pan, pour off the rendered fat and reserve, leaving just enough fat in the pan with the bacon to glaze the surface.
2. TO MAKE THE EASY SPICED BLACK BEANS: In a saucepan, heat the beans gently in their liquid. Stir in the cumin, chili powder, salt, and coffee. Add the bacon fat to the beans.
3. Put the skillet over low heat and quickly scramble the eggs with the bacon in the bacon fat until just softly set, about 2 minutes. While eggs are still soft, remove the pan from the heat and gently fold in the cheese. Set aside.

4. Working quickly, heat a large, dry cast-iron skillet over medium-high heat. Add the tortilla to the hot pan and cook until there is just a hint of crispiness on the bottom but the top is still pliable, about 90 seconds. (Do not flip the tortilla.)
5. Transfer the tortilla, crisp-side down, to a clean work surface and quickly spoon the eggs into the center, leaving a border of at least 2 in/5 cm uncovered for folding. Fold up the top and bottom edges of the tortilla to meet over the eggs, and then fold in the right and left sides. Turn the packet over and place on a plate, seam-side down.
6. Serve immediately with the spicy beans and pico de gallo alongside.

You will have enough black beans for about 6 servings.

Fried Taylor Pork Roll, Egg, and Cheese Sandwiches

Here's a classic breakfast sandwich with a local twist: layers of savory Taylor pork roll (a Philadelphia favorite, available online) and fried eggs with crispy edges under a velvety cap of melted cheese. It comes wrapped in foil, which tends to soften the roll, and is wolfed on the go. But it's just as good on a lightly toasted kaiser, eaten somewhere other than your car.

SERVES

1

(multiply for as many as you are willing to make)

LEVEL *of* **DIFFICULTY**

WORTH THE EFFORT

REASONABLE

EASY

2 or 3 slices Taylor pork roll
1 tsp unsalted butter
2 large eggs
2 slices American cheese
1 kaiser roll, split and lightly toasted

1. In a nonstick skillet over medium heat, fry the pork-roll slices until lightly browned. Remove from the heat and set aside.

2. Lower the heat and melt the butter in the same pan. Break the eggs into the melted butter and cover, frying until the eggs are set hard, 2 to 3 minutes. Remove the lid and place the pork slices and cheese over the eggs. Cover and cook until the cheese melts into a smooth dome.

3. Transfer to the kaiser roll, folding to fit. Serve immediately.

TIP

For big groups, fry all of the pork roll first and set aside on a paper towel–lined tray. As you make the sandwiches, keep them warm on a baking sheet in a low (200°F/93°C) oven. Hand them out when the coffee's ready.

Sautéed Wild Mushrooms with Eggs

Coming from New York, I was in culture shock when I got to Oregon and discovered this crazy abundance of affordable wild mushrooms. There are times during the peak mushroom season when it seems like there are more foragers in the restaurant trying to sell me wild mushrooms than there are customers. Although foraging was once a survival skill, today it's a solid way to connect with nature and practice local food sourcing. It's an easy thing to get into, but like any lost art, you have to learn from people who know what they're doing. Spotting wild mushrooms takes experience. Certain kinds grow under specific conditions, like morels that spring up after a forest fire. But in general, the Northwestern climate is ideal: plenty of rain soaking into the ground to create damp, mossy spots and rotting wood—the perfect wild-mushroom habitat.

Forage at your local greenmarket and even some quality supermarkets—they're getting so much better at stocking local produce these days. I can't tell you exactly what to buy because the mix in this salad depends on what you find. Just as the unpredictable is part of the fun of foraging in the woods, it's part of the fun of the dish. I heartily encourage you to combine as many as four or five kinds, if you can—the best plan is to let the mushroom medley be the star. The addition of herbs here bumps up the savory quality of the lettuce, and the crisp greens give you a great contrast to the richness of the eggs…but it's really all about the mushrooms. That's the whole point.

SERVES

10

LEVEL *of* **DIFFICULTY**

WORTH THE EFFORT

REASONABLE

EASY

DRESSING
2 shallots, minced
2 tbsp Champagne vinegar
2 tbsp Dijon mustard
2 tbsp warm water
2 tbsp honey
2 cups/480 ml grapeseed oil
Coarse salt and freshly ground black pepper

MUSHROOMS
3 tbsp grapeseed oil
4 lb/1.8 kg mixed wild mushrooms, trimmed and brushed clean
Coarse salt and freshly ground black pepper
3 shallots, minced

3 tsp fresh thyme leaves, finely chopped
6 tbsp/85 g unsalted butter

10 large eggs, cooked sunny-side up or scrambled*
4 lb/1.8 kg super-fresh small lettuces
1 cup/120 g pine nuts, toasted in a dry skillet just until you can smell them
1 bunch chives, snipped into bits
Leaves of 1 bunch fresh tarragon, torn into small pieces
Sea salt for sprinkling
Aged balsamic vinegar for drizzling
Crusty bread and prosciutto slices for serving →

Making ten fried eggs all at once can be challenging. Use a nonstick pan, and cook the eggs sunny-side up, one at a time. As they are done, transfer the eggs to a baking sheet in a 150°F/65°C oven; this will keep them warm without overcooking them. After the last egg is cooked, they can all go on the salads, still fresh and warm. Or, you could just make a big scramble.

1. TO MAKE THE DRESSING:
In a bowl, whisk together the shallots, vinegar, mustard, warm water, and honey. Slowly pour in the oil, whisking until emulsified. Season with salt and pepper. Set aside.

2. TO MAKE THE MUSHROOMS:
In the largest skillet you own, heat the oil over high heat to the point just before it smokes—the oil will shimmer in the pan. Add the mushrooms and spread them evenly around the pan, leaving a few gaps so the steam can escape. Cook, undisturbed (don't stir, and don't shake the pan—you want a proper sear), until browned, 6 to 8 minutes. Stir, flipping the mushrooms around; season with salt and pepper; and cook until browned on all sides, another 6 minutes or so. Add the shallots, thyme, and butter and lower the heat to medium. Cook until the butter melts and the shallots soften, about 5 minutes longer. Remove from the heat and let rest for about 5 minutes. Transfer the warm mushrooms to a large bowl.

3. Cook the eggs as desired and keep warm.

4. Add the lettuces, pine nuts, chives, tarragon, and about 1 cup/ 240 ml of the dressing to the bowl of mushrooms and toss gently to mix. Taste and adjust the seasoning with salt and pepper.

5. Divide the mushrooms-and-greens mixture among serving plates, and top each with an egg. Finish each plate with a sprinkling of sea salt and a drizzle of balsamic vinegar. Serve with a hunk of bread and a slice of prosciutto.

TIP

This dressing recipe makes about 2½ cups/600 ml. Use half for this dish and keep the rest in the refrigerator in a glass jar with a tight-fitting lid for up to 10 days. It can turn any hum-ho green salad into something special.

Breakfast Casserole with Sausage, Leeks, and Gruyère

In its heyday, cream of mushroom soup was used less as a soup and more as a convenient white sauce. No need to make a roux or chop mushrooms—Campbell's could turn any homemaker into what people called a "gourmet cook," adding a creamy, unctuous quality to the most basic casserole. It was a timesaver but also a flavor enhancer, even making ordinary white rice taste like risotto. My mom had her own special chicken dish that called for the trifecta of condensed soup: chicken, celery, and mushroom. I still ask her to make it for me when I go home to visit.

Today, as traceability and sourcing of ingredients becomes more and more important to me, Campbell's has status as a revered relic in my home kitchen. When I use it, I do so for fun and because it reminds me of another time. In its own weird way, it will always taste satisfyingly familiar, and that's what makes it good.

SERVES

16

LEVEL of DIFFICULTY

WORTH THE EFFORT

REASONABLE

EASY

CUSTARD
12 large eggs
4 cups/960 ml whole milk
1 cup/240 ml heavy cream
Two 10¾-oz/305-g cans cream of
    mushroom soup
1 tsp dry mustard
½ tsp coarse salt
¼ tsp freshly ground black pepper

16 to 20 slices challah bread (½ in/
    12 mm thick)
4 tbsp/55 g unsalted butter, softened
2 lb/910 g pork breakfast sausage,
    removed from casings and crumbled
¼ cup/60 ml olive oil
8 leeks, white and light green parts
    only, thinly sliced (see Tip, page 33)

¼ cup/10 g minced fresh herbs, such
    as a mixture of parsley, chives, and
    tarragon
8 cups/900 g shredded Gruyère cheese
Coarse salt and freshly ground
    black pepper
1 cup/115 g finely grated Parmesan cheese

TOPPING
1 lb/455 g thick-sliced applewood-smoked
    bacon, cut into ½-in/12-mm dice
2 lb/910 g cremini mushrooms, brushed
    clean and quartered
4 garlic cloves, minced
Coarse salt and freshly ground black pepper
¼ cup/10 g minced fresh herbs, such
    as a mixture of parsley, chives, and
    tarragon →

1. TO MAKE THE CUSTARD:
In a medium bowl, whisk together all of the custard ingredients. Set aside.

2. Preheat the oven to 350°F/180°C.

3. Arrange the challah slices on a large rimmed baking sheet and bake until lightly crisped and golden, about 10 minutes, turning the slices halfway through. Spread one side of the toasted bread slices with the softened butter. Cut the bread into 1-in/2.5-cm cubes and place in a large mixing bowl.

4. In a skillet over medium heat, cook the sausage, stirring and breaking up any clumps with a wooden spoon, until no longer pink, 5 to 7 minutes. Using a slotted spoon, transfer to the bowl with the bread.

5. Wipe out the skillet with a paper towel. Place over medium heat and add the olive oil. When the oil is hot, add the leeks and sauté until softened and fragrant, 3 to 4 minutes. Add to the bread mixture. Add the minced herbs, 6 cups/675 g of the Gruyère, a pinch of salt, and a few grinds of pepper and toss to mix well.

6. Pour the custard over the bread mixture and combine gently but thoroughly. You want the bread cubes to sit for a few minutes and drink up the custard until there aren't any dry spots. (If you're making the casserole for brunch, you can cover the bowl and refrigerate overnight.)

7. Butter two 9-by-13-in/23-by-33-cm or 10-by-15-in/25-by-38-cm glass or ceramic baking dishes (like a lasagna pan). Transfer the bread mixture to the prepared baking dishes, scatter the remaining Gruyère all over the tops, and sprinkle with the Parmesan. Place on a large rimmed baking sheet or sheets (to catch any spillage) and bake until browned and bubbly on top, 35 to 40 minutes.

8. MEANWHILE, MAKE THE TOPPING: Sauté the bacon in a skillet over medium-high heat until just crisp, about 8 minutes. Using a slotted spoon, transfer the bacon to paper towels to drain, leaving the rendered fat in the skillet. Add the mushrooms to the pan and sauté over medium heat until just soft, 3 to 4 minutes. Add the garlic and sauté until aromatic, 1 to 2 minutes longer. Lightly season the mushrooms with salt and pepper, then stir in the bacon and 2 tbsp of the extra minced herbs. Set aside and cover to keep warm.

9. Top each serving with a large spoonful of the mushrooms and garnish using the remaining 2 tbsp herbs.

TIP

The tight layers of mature leeks are typically filled with grit that is elusive to wash water, making them a little tricky to prep. An easy way to clean leeks: chop or slice as called for in your recipe (whole leeks are a story for another time), then transfer to a bowl—ideally a salad spinner—of water. Swish the leeks thoroughly in the water, loosening up the rings as you swish. Let sit for a few minutes so the dirt can settle, then lift them out with your hands to a kitchen towel to drain or drain from the salad spinner, leaving the dirt behind in the bowl. Repeat for extra-gritty leeks. Pat or spin dry thoroughly.

Late Afternoon

BRYAN CASWELL | REEF | *Houston, Texas*

Oven-Roasted Oysters

SERVES

6

LEVEL *of* **DIFFICULTY**

WORTH THE EFFORT

REASONABLE

EASY

The coastal culture of the South is a part of who I am as a person and as a chef. If it swims in the Gulf of Mexico, I've caught it and cooked it, and that goes for oysters, too. Some of my earliest memories are of my father taking me fishing out in the Gulf, off the coast of Texas. As we fished, we would eat raw oysters by the dozen, with a dash of hot sauce.

For a lot of people, though, oysters are a little (or a lot) special. You order them at steakhouses or have them in seafood towers. With a martini, maybe. I'm all for that, but roast some at home and you'll get a little closer to understanding everyday life in a fishing community.

I think people need to understand the impact of the water where the oyster lives. Oysters are the most sustainable food because they truly are what they eat—right down to the mineral content, the salinity, and the temperature of the water pumped through their gills. Don't let the difference in their size and shape throw you; from Maine on down to the Gulf, all native East Coast oysters are the same species: *Crassostrea virginica.* What distinguishes them is their watery home. Oysters from colder water are firmer, with a flinty, mineral-like taste, perfect for eating on the half shell. But Gulf oysters are sweeter and meatier, with deep-cup shells and more liquor, so they don't dry out when you apply heat. (I like to showcase local seafood at my restaurants, and I'm especially proud of the oysters from the newly revitalized Galveston Bay. But if you can't get your hands on Texas oysters, you'll also get good results roasting larger cold-water oysters, like Blue Points.)

We roast more oysters at the restaurant than you can imagine, and our method also works at home. To help keep the oysters moist, we roast them on a bed of hot rock salt that allows each oyster to cook with equal heat from above and below, steaming in its own juices without drying out. Whether you're roasting oysters or just eating them on the half shell, serving them on a bed of rock salt keeps the oysters level, so they don't tip over and lose any of their liquor—that's pure flavor. At this point, a martini is optional. I usually crack open a Shiner Bock.

(a)   (b)   (c)   (d)

COCKTAIL SAUCE*

One 12-oz/340-g jar Heinz chili sauce

3 tbsp grated fresh horseradish, or more if you are stout-hearted (you can also use prepared horseradish, available in refrigerated jars at the supermarket)

2 tbsp Worcestershire sauce

6 to 8 cups/840 g to 1.1 kg rock salt

36 oysters, preferably Texas Gulf or large cold-water varieties

Hot sauce, such as Crystal, for serving**

1. TO MAKE THE COCKTAIL SAUCE: In a medium bowl, stir together the chili sauce, horseradish, and Worcestershire. Place the bowl in the refrigerator to chill until ready to serve.

2. Crank the oven to 425°F/220°C. Fill a roasting pan halfway with the rock salt.

3. Rinse the oysters, scrubbing them free of mud and sand, and set them aside. Do not dry—in the hot oven, the excess moisture will create steam that loosens the hinge muscle, making the oyster easier to open.

4. Put the roasting pan in the oven and heat until the rock salt is crazy hot, about 15 minutes. Nestle the damp oysters, deep-cup-side down, in the hot rock salt. (Don't overcrowd, as they need air circulation.) **(a)** Return the pan to the oven and roast until the tension on the hinge seals is released and the oysters open slightly, 6 to 8 minutes. Remove from the oven. Discard any that do not open at all.

5. (b) Working with one oyster at a time and using a folded kitchen towel, hold each oyster level (so you don't lose any liquid) and open with an oyster knife (or, in a pinch, we've used a paring knife, with care). **(c)** First, hold the knife curved-side down, tracing the upper shell, cutting the adductor muscle, and removing the top shell. (Discard the tops.) Then go curved-side up along the bottom, again severing the adductor, to loosen the meat from the shell. Many oyster knives are gently curved in order to follow the shape of the shell. It is an easy process.

6. (d) Leave the oyster sitting in the bottom shell and arrange the shucked oysters back in the pan of rock salt. Serve immediately with the cold cocktail sauce and a drop of hot sauce.

Serve the sauce in small portions, keeping backup containers in the refrigerator so it is always fresh and cold. (Small ramekins work well. They are often sold in multipacks at kitchen-supply stores and are also useful for individual servings of jam, syrup, and salt.) This recipe makes about 1½ cups/360 ml and will keep well in the refrigerator for up to 2 weeks.

Louisiana Crystal Hot Sauce is mild enough to let the flavor of the oysters shine through, or try Sriracha.

Shrimp Kabobs

I like to serve food that everyone can just pick at and snack on while they're watching the game. A few years ago, twenty or so people gathered at my house to watch my beloved Giants upset the favorites from New England. I set out bowls of munchies, platters of salami—things people could easily grab.

Use good-size shrimp for this recipe so they cook evenly along with the fennel and onion—ask your fishmonger for U-16s (that means there are 16 or fewer to a pound). The tender citrus-marinated shellfish and crunchy anise-flavored fennel is a good way to get both texture and taste on a single skewer. And unlike Eli Manning's throw to David Tyree in the final moments of Super Bowl XLII in 2008, food on a stick is pretty easy to grab.

SERVES

10

(or 12 as an appetizer)

LEVEL *of* **DIFFICULTY**

WORTH THE EFFORT

REASONABLE

EASY

MARINADE
2½ cups/600 ml orange juice
2½ tbsp fresh lemon juice
1½ cups/360 ml olive oil
Coarse salt and freshly ground
black pepper

2 fennel bulbs
48 large shrimp, peeled and deveined
2 red onions, cut into thick strips

1. Gather 16 metal or wooden skewers. If you're using wooden skewers, soak them in water for 1 hour before loading them. This prevents them from burning during grilling.
2. TO MAKE THE MARINADE: Whisk together the citrus juices and olive oil. Season with salt and pepper and set aside.
3. Bring a small saucepan of water to a boil. Meanwhile, cut off the tops of the fennel bulbs (save the feathery fronds for salads, garnishes, or other uses, if you like) and cut out and discard the tough core. Cut the bulb into sticks. Add to the boiling water and blanch for 1 minute. Drain and let cool.
4. Load the shrimp, fennel, and onion onto the skewers, putting three shrimp

and two or three pieces of each vegetable on each and alternating them so they look good. Place the assembled kabobs in a shallow container. Pour the marinade evenly over the kabobs. Cover tightly with plastic wrap and refrigerate for at least 2 hours before grilling.
5. Build a medium-hot fire in a charcoal grill or preheat a gas grill to medium.
6. Discard the marinade and plop the kabobs on the grill. Grill in batches, if needed; you don't want to crowd the rack. Cook, turning every minute or so to hit all sides, until the shrimp turn pink and the vegetables develop a slight char. Pile them on a large platter and serve immediately.

TIP

You can load the kabobs and start marinating them a day ahead. They will become more flavorful the longer they marinate. The kabobs don't have to be served hot. You can grill them an hour before people arrive and serve them at room temperature.

Ceviche

I'm from Kent Island in the Chesapeake Bay, so I'm accustomed to getting my hands on the freshest fish imaginable. There's no need to do much to fish when it's fresh, so I often turn it into ceviche, a dish that originated in the coastal cultures of Latin and Central America. Raw fish is soaked in an acid-based liquid—usually citrus juice is the main ingredient—which denatures the proteins, a process that changes the texture of the fish, leaving the interior opaque and the edges firm, almost as if heat had been applied. (People say in shorthand that it "cooks" the fish.) Ceviche is man's best seafood friend because it's a showy dish that's easy to make and rich enough to serve in small amounts, like this first-course salad. Using striped bass from the Chesapeake, I add traditional flavors from southern Italy—another of my favorite coastal regions. If stripers aren't coming out of your local waters, you can use another firm-fleshed fish with a mild, sweet flavor, like red snapper or black bass. Have the fishmonger skin the fish or do it yourself. All it takes is practice and a sharp blade, and you'll be gliding.

SERVES

4

LEVEL *of*
DIFFICULTY

WORTH
THE EFFORT

REASONABLE

EASY

1 small fennel bulb

1 blood orange

One 12- to 14-oz/340- to 400-g
  boneless fillet of striped bass,
  skinned (see page 41) and
  cut into ¼-in/6-mm dice

2 tbsp fresh lemon juice

1 tbsp fresh tangerine juice

Sea salt and freshly ground black
  pepper

2 tbsp good-quality olive oil

8 mild oil-cured green olives such as
  Castelvetrano olives, pitted and
  cut into quarters

2 tbsp capers, rinsed and drained

6 fresh mint leaves, torn or snipped
  into ribbons →

TIP

*Prep the salad
ingredients first so
you aren't rushing
through them during
the fish's short
marinating time.*

1. Cut off the top of the fennel bulb. Coarsely chop about 1 tbsp of the feathery fronds and set aside. Pick another 8 small sprigs, but leave them whole and set aside. Discard the top. Peel off the fennel bulb's tough outer layer, cut out and discard the core. Slice the bulb as thinly as you can and set aside.

2. Using a sharp chef's knife and following the contour of the fruit, cut off the peel and as much of the bitter white pith underneath as possible from the orange. Cut four ¼-in/6-mm crosswise slices from the orange and cut each slice in half to form eight half-moon pieces. Set aside, along with the remaining orange.

3. Place the fish in a bowl and toss gently with the lemon juice, tangerine juice, and a pinch each of salt and pepper. Mix very well. Refrigerate for about 5 minutes. The mixture should have thickened and coated the fish, and the fish should be whiter in color. Give it a few more minutes, if not.

4. When the fish is ready, remove from the refrigerator and fold in the sliced fennel, the chopped fennel fronds, 1½ tbsp of the olive oil, the olives, capers, and mint.

5. Spoon the ceviche into a serving dish. Squeeze in the juice from the reserved uncut blood orange. Drizzle the remaining ½ tbsp olive oil over the top and garnish with the orange pieces and fennel sprigs. Sprinkle with a little more salt. Eat now.

HOW TO

SKIN A FISH

↓

Buying skin-on fish lets you see how it was treated, because you can check the skin for blemishes or discoloration. It should be shiny and smooth. Skin also protects the delicate flesh from direct contact with ice displays.

STEP 1

Without cutting through the skin, make a cut about ½ in/12 mm from the tail end straight down.

STEP 2

Angle the heel of the blade about 20 degrees while holding the tail end with your other hand. Using a fluid motion, pull the knife toward you from heel to tip while moving down the fillet.

STEP 3

As the knife moves away from the tail end, use your other hand to gently pull the flesh up and away from the skin as you slice.

STEP 4

After you've completed a stroke, lift the fish, place the heel of the knife at the point where the skin and fish are still joined, and start again, using long smooth slices. (Pinkie extension optional.)

FRANCINE MAROUKIAN AND TONY AIAZZI | THE WORKSHOP KITCHEN | *Philadelphia, Pennsylvania*

Clams Casino Stew

Rhode Island's classic clams casino, often credited to Julius Keller, maître d' at the original Narragansett Pier Casino, is a baked half-shell appetizer traditionally made with shoreline flavor elements: clams, bacon, vegetables, and breading. This one-pot interpretation is assembled in two parts: routine stove-top prep and grand grill finale.

SERVES

(as an appetizer or light lunch)

LEVEL *of* DIFFICULTY

WORTH THE EFFORT

REASONABLE

EASY

Sea salt

4 dozen littleneck clams, scrubbed

4 thick strips bacon, cut crosswise into ½-in/12-mm strips

1 yellow onion, diced

6 garlic cloves, sliced

Three-finger pinch of red pepper flakes

1 cup/240 ml dry white wine

2 tbsp unsalted butter

½ lemon, visible seeds removed

GARLIC BREAD

1 large garlic clove, chopped or put through a garlic press

3 tbsp unsalted butter, softened

1 tbsp olive oil

Good pinch of coarse salt

Few good shakes of paprika

1 baguette, split lengthwise

1½ tsp chopped fresh herbs such as chives, rosemary, or parsley, or a mixture

½ cup/15 g coarsely chopped fresh parsley →

1. Build a hot fire in a charcoal grill or preheat a gas grill to high.

2. Prepare a large bowl of cold water with enough sea salt added so that it tastes like seawater. Submerge the clams in the water and let sit for about 20 minutes to allow the clams to circulate water through themselves and release silt. Transfer the clams to a bowl and set aside. Discard the soaking liquid and any open clams that don't close when you touch them.

3. In a Dutch oven or other pot with a tight-fitting lid large enough to hold all the clams, cook the bacon over medium heat until crisp. Using a slotted spoon, transfer to paper towels to drain. Add the onion, garlic, and red pepper flakes to the bacon fat in the pot, stir to coat, and cook until the onion is just tender, 2 to 3 minutes. Add the wine and butter. Squeeze in the juice from the lemon and drop the rind into the pot. Bring to a simmer, stirring. Let simmer until reduced slightly, about 5 minutes. Remove from the heat and cover to keep warm until you're ready to cook the clams.

4. **TO MAKE THE GARLIC BREAD:** Combine the garlic, butter, olive oil, salt, and paprika in a small bowl and mash together with a fork into a smooth spread. Spread the butter evenly onto the cut sides of the bread, sprinkle with the herbs, and close the baguette halves like a sandwich, pressing lightly to seal. Wrap securely in aluminum foil. Cook the bread on the cooler part of the grill, turning occasionally. (Cut in half or even smaller pieces if you have a round grill.) Poke the bread with your fingers to test for doneness. Although it will feel soft at first because the butter is steaming, after about 10 minutes the bread should feel a little crisp to the touch. Open the foil packets and grill the buttered sides of the bread lightly to toast. Rewrap the bread in foil to keep warm while you cook the clams.

5. Place the Dutch oven on the grill over high heat. Add the clams and re-cover. Occasionally give the pot a shake (this helps the clams to open), but do not uncover for at least 10 minutes, as the steam cooks the clams and forces the shells open. Discard any clams that remain closed.

6. When all the clams have opened, divide them among soup plates and ladle the hot cooking liquid over the top. Sprinkle with the bacon and parsley and serve immediately, with hunks of garlic bread.

Cooking on the Beach

JEREMY SEWALL, ISLAND CREEK OYSTER BAR

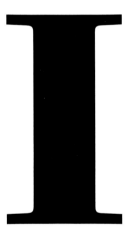

I COME FROM a family of lobstermen. Growing up, we would have big clambakes on the beach, with lobsters caught that morning. You can re-create this pretty much anywhere with a classic New England bonfire. Dig a hole in the sand or dirt, 1 ft/30.5 cm deep and 2½ ft/76 cm square. Build a big fire inside. Use hardwood if you have it—apple, oak, birch. Wait until the flames burn down and you have a bed of really, really hot coals.

First thing to do is get some potatoes going. They take about an hour. Wrap each one in foil and set them around the edge of the fire, right in the coals. Flip them a couple of times as they cook. Next, prop a grill grate about 8 in/ 20 cm above the coals. Put a few sticks of butter in a flameproof pot and set it toward the edge of the grate so the butter melts while you get the fish ready. (Keep your seafood on a layer of ice in a cooler until you're ready to cook, but never let the ice melt so much that your clams or lobsters are in standing water. They'll drown.) Lay hard-shelled clams like littlenecks or cherrystones directly on the grill and let them open up. Grab them off the grill with tongs and dip them in the melted butter. You can do the same thing with oysters, minus the butter.

Split live lobsters in half lengthwise by laying each one on its back and driving the tip of a knife through the head—this kills them instantly. Then just continue cutting down the length of the lobster. Crack the claws a little so the meat gets exposed to the heat—claw shells are thicker than the rest of the body. Throw the lobster halves on the grill and turn them while they cook. When the tail meat is nice and white and feels firm, the lobster is cooked.

There are no rules to this. Let everyone graze around the fire all afternoon and into the night. You'll have some fresh lemon you're squeezing on everything. Everyone will be eating with their hands. And you'll never want it to stop.

Portuguese Fisherman's Stew

It all started in the late 1970s, when I was searching for an identity as a young chef. I knew I was never going to be French, so I focused my research right where I lived—New England, not just the classic "well-bred" dishes but also regional stuff. Living in Boston meant I was already working with a lot of Portuguese cooks; in time, I began to understand the accent of their cooking.

For the next twenty years or so, I was a fine-dining chef, but my real fantasy was always to have a clam shack—the sort of shore food found on the boardwalk and in funky taverns. This stew is the melding of my two careers in one pot.

In the same way salt pork or bacon bolsters chowder, chorizo adds a little fat to an otherwise lean dish, and the spices drift out during cooking, flavoring the broth. Meanwhile, the acidity of the wine and tomatoes cuts through the richness of the sausage. The list of ingredients may be long, but put them together and let the stew do what it's designed to do—cook itself.

SERVES

12

LEVEL *of*
DIFFICULTY

WORTH
THE EFFORT

REASONABLE

EASY

¾ cup/180 ml olive oil

8 small bay leaves

1 tsp red pepper flakes

6 garlic cloves, minced

Leaves from 8 sprigs fresh thyme, chopped

3 medium yellow onions, thinly sliced

3 medium red or green bell peppers, seeded and thinly sliced

2 tsp saffron threads, chopped

Three 14-oz/400-g cans whole tomatoes, strained, juice reserved and tomatoes cut into strips

3 cups/720 ml dry white wine

6 cups/1.4 L fish stock, clam juice, chicken stock, or water

12 oz/340 g chorizo or linguiça sausage, removed from casings and sliced ½ in/12 mm thick

24 littleneck clams, scrubbed

24 oz/680 g lean fish fillets such as hake, cod, halibut, or striped bass, cut into 12 pieces

24 oz/680 g fatty fish fillets such as bluefish or mackerel, skin and blood line (the spongy dark strip found in fast-swimming fish) removed and discarded, cut into 12 pieces

30 oz/850 g mussels, scrubbed and debearded (see facing page)

12 oz/340 g squid, including tentacles, cleaned and bodies cut into rings about ½ in/12 mm thick*

Kosher or coarse salt and freshly ground black pepper

⅓ cup/10 g packed fresh flat-leaf parsley leaves, chopped

⅓ cup/10 g packed fresh cilantro leaves, chopped

6 cups/570 g cooked white or brown rice

✴ *Don't try to clean the squid yourself, unless you're excited about trying; just ask your fishmonger to do it.*

1. In a very large (10- to 12-qt/2.4- to 2.8-L) heavy-bottomed pot, heat the olive oil over medium heat. Add the bay leaves and red pepper flakes and sauté until sizzling and the bay leaves begin to brown, about 1 minute. Add the garlic, thyme, onions, and bell peppers and sauté, stirring often, until the vegetables are softened but not browned, about 10 minutes. Stir in the saffron and sauté until fragrant, about 2 minutes.

2. Add the tomatoes and their juices, the wine, and fish stock and raise the heat to medium-high. Bring to a boil, stirring once or twice. Stir in the chorizo and clams, discarding any open clams that don't close when you touch them. Simmer, uncovered, for 4 minutes. Add the lean and fatty fish and stir to submerge while still raw. Simmer slowly for about 10 minutes, lowering the heat if the stew seems to be boiling too fast. Add the mussels and squid, this time leaving them on top of the stew without submerging (the steam will cook them), and simmer for 6 minutes longer. Remove from the heat and let sit for 20 minutes to allow the flavors to blend.

3. Using tongs, evenly distribute the fish and shellfish among 12 soup plates or bowls. (Discard any clams or mussels that failed to open.) Return the broth to low heat, season with salt and pepper, and stir in the parsley and cilantro. Ladle the hot broth over the seafood in each bowl and serve immediately, passing the rice at the table.

TIP

Have everything chopped, measured, and ready before you start.

HOW TO
CLEAN MUSSELS

↓

Wild mussels (as opposed to farmed) come with their protective tuft attached, a firm but stretchy network of fibers called byssus threads by which mussels anchor themselves to rocks for protection against wave forces. This is called the beard. You have to take it off before you cook. So, rinse the mussels under cool water. Give any open shell a strong finger flick to see if it closes. If it doesn't, it's dead. Throw it away and move on. Pick up a mussel with one hand and grab the beard with the other. Don't let go. Wiggle it back and forth to pull it out of the shell as much as possible. Pull the beard back toward the hinge and break it off, using the back of a paring knife as a fulcrum if necessary. Scrub the mussel shells free of any debris or clinging algae. Mussels don't burrow into the sand like clams, so they won't be loaded with grit, but you want the broth to be silky clean.

STEVEN SATTERFIELD | **MILLER UNION** | *Atlanta, Georgia*

Lowcountry Boil

Every port city has a great seafood one-pot, and in my hometown of Savannah we have the Lowcountry Boil. Its supposed inventor, Richard Gay, whose family runs a fish company in the community of Frogmore on St. Helena Island, gave it its other name, Frogmore stew, which is weirdly misleading. What you have here is not a conventional stew, in which the cooking liquid becomes a rich sauce. In this case, the seasoned liquid is merely a means of getting flavor into the ingredients and providing a gentle way of cooking. Then it's all about the newspaper. Traditionally, this dish is served on big steaming platters set down on clean newspaper, which becomes the fish wrap for all your castoffs. Just eat and enjoy, plunking down your shrimp shells and corncobs—it'll only take a minute to roll up the newspaper and throw everything away. There are even places along the South Carolina coastline where you eat your Frogmore stew at long wooden tables that have a hole in the center, with a trash can underneath: Peel, throw, eat.

This is an ideal meal for a big crowd at a summer house. You can batch it up or down, depending on the size of the group—don't worry about perfectly portioning each ingredient. It's the cooking time for each ingredient that matters. That, and making sure there's enough beer.

SERVES

LEVEL of DIFFICULTY

WORTH THE EFFORT

REASONABLE

EASY

BROTH

2 gl/7.5 L water

Two 12-oz/360-ml bottles beer (whatever you're drinking while you prep)

½ cup/30 g Old Bay seasoning

3 tbsp kosher salt

2 bay leaves

6 large stalks celery, cut in half crosswise (inner leafy stalks are best)

3 lemons, quartered, visible seeds removed

2 Vidalia (sweet) onions, peeled and quartered but with root end intact (just rinse off the dirt and trim away the tap roots)

3 lb/1.4 kg small (about the size of ping-pong balls) red-skinned new potatoes, scrubbed but left whole*

2 ½ lb/1.2 kg smoked sausage such as andouille or kielbasa, cut on the diagonal into 1-in/2.5-cm pieces

4 mildly hot green chiles such as poblano, Anaheim, Cubanelle, or Hungarian wax, quartered and seeded

10 ears corn, shucked and cut crosswise into 2-in/5-cm chunks

5 to 6 lb/2.3 to 2.7 kg shrimp, preferably jumbo (usually 12 to 16 per 1 lb/455 g), in the shell

Cocktail Sauce (page 37) for serving

Warm French bread and butter for serving →

Poor but viable substitute in a pinch: medium russet potatoes, scrubbed and cut into halves or quarters.

1. TO MAKE THE BROTH: In a large stockpot, combine the broth ingredients, squeezing the juice of the lemons in before you toss in the rinds. Be sure to add the onions and potatoes while the liquid is cold. Bring the pot to a boil. Lower the heat to maintain a simmer.

2. After the broth has simmered for about 20 minutes, test the potatoes for doneness. They should be easily pierced with a knife but not mushy. Using a slotted spoon, spider, or tongs, remove the celery and lemons and discard. Transfer the onions and potatoes to a large colander placed in the sink.

3. Return the broth to a simmer, add the sausage and chiles, and cook for 5 minutes. Add the corn and cook for 5 minutes more. When you're ready to eat, gather the guests and then drop in the shrimp and cook for 3 minutes. Using the slotted spoon or spider, remove the shrimp as soon as they're cooked and distribute them equally among serving platters. Scoop out the sausage, chiles, and corn and distribute them among the platters, too.

4. Ladle some of the broth into small dipping bowls for the bread, then pour the remainder into the colander holding the onions and potatoes to rewarm them; drain well. Add the onions and potatoes to the platters. Serve the platters of boil on a table covered in clean newspaper, with the bowls of broth, cocktail sauce, and bread and butter.

When the shrimp are perfectly cooked, they will become shrimp-pink and float to the surface. That's when you remove them. Don't leave them in the broth longer or they will overcook.

First, You Need a Big Pot

TOM CHIARELLA

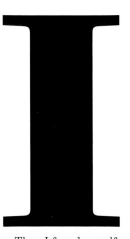

I'D NEVER CARED for food prepared on a massive family-reunion scale. Vast bowls of baked beans, elbow-deep pails of coleslaw, giant foil trays of chicken, even the smaller casseroles pitched in from afar. It's an overlarge task, and since everyone helps, no one is responsible. In this way, one Saturday starts to taste like any other.

Then I found myself renting a large house off the Carolina coast with a pack of friends. Nineteen or twenty people minimum, sometimes as many as thirty, every night. A lot of hamburgers, that—it was like Ann-Margret up in there with all the baked beans. The repetition was deadening. So when my turn came, I insisted on going solo. I dug through a cookbook, found a recipe for bouillabaisse. Then tripled it.

When you cook on a large scale, every rule is suspended, redefined, altered. I required equipment I never knew existed, had to rent a stockpot from a seafood place—a pot so big a baby could have slept in it. As I left, a black guy in kitchen whites jogged out after me, handing me a wooden spoon the size of a Little League baseball bat. "No charge," he told me. He looked at the food splayed across my backseat. "Cooking big, huh? That is hard. You gotta turn that soup over. And you don't need no heat at all. Just time."

The volume of food—the mussels, the clams, the fish and crab, the sacks of vegetables—scared me, and the money, pitched in from everyone, made me feel the responsibility in my ribs. I cooked all afternoon, attentive and focused as a librarian. Then at five o'clock, thinking I was due a break, I left things simmering, slipped into the hot tub, drank something icy, and congratulated myself for going the long way, on my own.

Thirty minutes. That was all. Even on the lowest heat, the bottom of the soup burned. And when the bottom of a soup burns, that char flavors the whole soup. I served it anyway. People were pleasant. They appreciated that I'd shot high. Still, it killed the room.

The time. The money. The promises. I learned every lesson I needed to learn in that one disaster: Cooking big is hard. Being attentive means staying that way until the food is on the table. Lose pretension. The volume of food means it's acceptable to make menu choices that might seem pedestrian but that are relatively easy to goose up. Chili, with Italian-style pork ribs added at the end. Corn bread, but with a little pancetta and sun-dried tomatoes. Like that. And don't go it alone when it isn't necessary. Cooking with others is a pleasure that pride should not impede.

On the night with the bouillabaisse, no one called me out. Eventually, someone pulled out some hot dogs—"for the kids"—and a container of leftover beans to reheat in the microwave. I didn't object. We drank wine. Some left my soup uneaten, others insisted it was great. Meanwhile the grill was lit, plates were set out. Even I helped. We were quick about it. It was a team effort.

DONALD LINK | COCHON | *New Orleans, Louisiana*

Gumbo

Although it varies from cook to cook, gumbo is south Louisiana's signature dish—a complex stew thickened by a roux, a mixture of fat and flour that's carefully cooked into a paste with color ranging from blond to dark brown, depending on what's going into the pot. When I was growing up, we had chicken-and-sausage gumbo or seafood gumbo, but it was rare to find a combination of the two—probably because the smoked sausage there can be a bit overpowering. However, in this gumbo made with chicken, shrimp, and tasso—spicy smoked pork that's a staple of south Louisiana cooking—the three ingredients complement one another because the distinctive flavor of tasso provides good balance, keeping the shrimp and chicken on an even playing field.

Maybe you've heard that only little old ladies in Louisiana know how to make a roux. That's not totally true. But it does take care and attention. I generally make my roux somewhat lighter for gumbos that have seafood in them because it helps the flavor stand out, but even a lighter roux requires vigilance and constant whisking. One little bit of flour stuck to the bottom of the pot can burn, screwing up the flavor of the whole gumbo. Just remember to whisk slowly. They call roux "Cajun napalm" for good reason: If a flying drop lands on your skin, it'll give you a good sizzle. That shit hurts.

SERVES

10

LEVEL *of* **DIFFICULTY**

WORTH THE EFFORT

REASONABLE

EASY

GUMBO SPICE MIX

3 tsp kosher salt

1½ tsp freshly ground black pepper

1½ tsp cayenne pepper

1 tsp paprika

1 tsp dried thyme

1 tsp filé powder*

6 bay leaves

2 cups/480 ml vegetable oil

½ cup/60 g all-purpose flour, plus
  1¾ cups/215 g

2 tsp kosher salt

½ tsp black pepper

½ tsp paprika

4 boneless, skin-on chicken thighs,
  cut into 2-in/5-cm pieces

1 lb/455 g tasso,* diced

1 yellow onion, diced

3 stalks celery, diced

2 poblano chiles, seeded and diced

1 small jalapeño chile, seeded
  and diced

4 garlic cloves, minced

4 qt/3.8 L chicken stock

1 lb/455 g Louisiana shrimp, peeled
  and deveined

Steamed rice for serving

Potato salad for serving (optional) →

✳

With its historic mix of European and Afro-Caribbean cultures, New Orleans has some of the country's most unique indigenous cuisine. If filé powder (ground sassafras leaves) and tasso aren't available at your supermarket— although they may well be—order them from cajungrocer.com.

1. TO MAKE THE GUMBO SPICE MIX: In a small bowl, combine all the ingredients and stir. Set aside.

2. Heat the oil in a very large (2-gl/7.5-L) heavy-bottomed pot over medium-high heat until a tiny pinch of flour gently sizzles on contact.

3. While the oil is heating, stir together the ½ cup/60 g flour, salt, pepper, and paprika in a small bowl. Coat the chicken with the flour mixture, reserving the excess mixture. Fry the chicken pieces in the hot oil, turning once, until light golden brown on both sides, about 8 minutes total, then transfer to paper towels to drain. (The chicken does not have to be cooked through at this point.) Lower the heat to medium.

4. In a medium bowl, whisk together the remaining 1¾ cups/215 g flour and the flour mix remaining from coating the chicken. Start adding the flour to the hot oil a little at a time, whisking constantly. Once all of the flour has been added, stir over medium heat until the roux is a deep honey brown, about 40 minutes.

5. Add the tasso, onion, celery, poblanos, jalapeño, garlic, and gumbo spice to the roux. Cook until the vegetables are slightly softened and the spices are blended, about 4 minutes. Stir in the chicken stock and bring to a simmer, being sure to scrape the bottom of the pot as the gumbo comes to a simmer so the roux doesn't stick. Simmer until thickened, about 30 minutes, stirring often and skimming all the fat that rises to the surface. (It might be a lot, like five or six ladlesful.)

6. Add the chicken and shrimp and simmer for 45 minutes longer, again skimming any fat that floats to the top. Taste (carefully). (Some tasso is spicier than others—if you want more heat, add another ½ tsp cayenne and another 1 tsp salt.)

7. Ladle the gumbo into soup plates or bowls and serve immediately with steamed rice and potato salad on the side. (I dip potato salad in my gumbo.) You can also let it cool, refrigerate, and then reheat gently to serve the next day.

Chef Link's signature hot sauce pulls together the flavors in his gumbo— or yours. Order it at cochon butcher.com.

Wild Boar Chili

My parents are from India, but I was born and raised in Kentucky, where we know all about giant wild pigs.

SERVES

LEVEL *of* DIFFICULTY

WORTH THE EFFORT

REASONABLE

EASY

GARAM MASALA*
One 3-in/7.5-cm stick cinnamon
2 tbsp cumin seeds
2 tbsp coriander seeds
2 tbsp cardamom pods
2 tbsp black peppercorns
2 tbsp red pepper flakes
½ tsp whole cloves
½ tsp freshly grated nutmeg

¼ cup/60 ml olive oil
3 lb/1.4 kg wild boar leg, ground
1 lb/455 g pork shoulder, ground twice (ask your butcher to do this)
1 strip thick bacon, minced
Coarse salt and freshly ground black pepper
1 large yellow onion, minced
4 garlic cloves, minced
1 jalapeño chile, seeded and minced
2 tbsp tomato paste
2 qt/910 g sweet cherry tomatoes, halved
2 cups/480 ml chicken stock
Two 15-oz/430-g cans red kidney beans, rinsed and drained
Chopped fresh cilantro for garnish

1. TO MAKE THE GARAM MASALA: In a small, dry skillet over medium heat, combine all of the ingredients and toast, stirring often, until slightly browned and very aromatic, about 2 minutes. Transfer to a plate and let cool. Grind in a spice grinder, a coffee grinder reserved for that use, or a blender. Measure out ¼ cup/30 g and set aside.

2. In a large, heavy-bottomed pot over medium-high heat, heat the olive oil until nearly smoking. Add the boar, pork, and bacon. Season with salt and pepper, and cook, stirring and breaking up any clumps with your spoon, until deeply and evenly browned, about 15 minutes.

3. Add the onion, garlic, and jalapeño to the pot. Season with salt and pepper, lower the heat to medium, and cook until the vegetables are softened, 6 to 8 minutes. Add the tomato paste and cook, stirring often, for about 5 minutes. Add the cherry tomatoes, cover, and cook about 20 minutes. Stir in the garam masala and the stock and simmer until well combined, about 5 minutes. Stir in the beans and cook until the juices are slightly thickened, about 30 minutes longer. Serve garnished with the cilantro.

Alternative to all this: Storebought garam masala. You will only use about half of the garam masala you make; store the rest in a tightly sealed jar in a cool, dark place.

BRYAN VOLTAGGIO | RANGE | *Washington, D.C.*

Cabin Fever Chili

Chili is a romantic idea—you throw in a little of this and a little of that on a winter's afternoon, and eventually everyone gathers around and says how delicious it is. But while you don't need to be obsessive about measurements, it is possible to screw up chili. That's why chili recipes exist. Still, it would be nice to be able to put a great chili together without poring over a cookbook, which is why I've created a template. (See pages 60–61 for a rough outline of how, exactly, a great batch of chili is constructed, to encourage improvisation. Why? Because there are few more personal dishes than chili, and you should develop yours.) Below is a recipe you can follow to the letter. These quantities may be quadrupled (use two stockpots) and the proportions will remain perfectly balanced.

SERVES

LEVEL *of* **DIFFICULTY**

WORTH THE EFFORT

REASONABLE

EASY

1 cup/225 g diced applewood-smoked bacon
1 lb/455 g ground beef
1 lb/455 g ground pork

VEGETABLE MIX
1 yellow onion, minced
1 red bell pepper, seeded and diced
1 yellow bell pepper, seeded and diced
4 garlic cloves, minced

SPICE MIX
3 tbsp dark chili powder (a rich and fruity blend, such as McCormick's, can be found in grocery stores)
1 tbsp ground cumin
1 tbsp ground chipotle chile powder
1 tbsp dried oregano
1 tbsp Spanish smoked paprika (the sweet version, not the hot)

1 tsp unsweetened cocoa powder
1½ tsp coarse salt
½ tsp freshly ground black pepper

One 15-oz/430-g can red kidney beans, rinsed and drained
One 15-oz/430-g can white navy beans, rinsed and drained
One 12-oz/360-ml bottle American lager
One 14½-oz/415-g can crushed tomatoes
One 14½-oz/415-g can diced tomatoes, with juice
Shredded Monterey Jack or Cheddar cheese for serving
Chopped fresh cilantro for serving
Chopped scallions for serving

1. In a large, heavy-bottomed Dutch oven, cook the bacon over medium heat, stirring occasionally, until lightly crisp. Add the beef and pork and brown, stirring occasionally and breaking up any clumps with your spoon, until nicely browned all sides, 10 to 12 minutes.
2. Add the Spice Mix and Vegetable Mix and cook until the vegetables are softened, stirring often to coat the meat and vegetables with the spices, about 5 minutes. Stir in the kidney beans, navy beans, and beer until combined. Add the crushed and diced tomatoes. Turn the heat to low and simmer very gently, stirring occasionally, for 1½ hours. Taste and adjust the seasoning.
3. Ladle the chili into soup bowls and sprinkle with the cheese, cilantro, and scallions, or pass them at the table. Serve immediately.

TURN THE PAGE TO FIND OUT HOW TO IMPROVISE

How to Pull Off Chili On Your Own

BRYAN VOLTAGGIO

Chili must always start with a recipe—the proportions are important. But once you get it down, you have to make it yours.

FAT

1 cup/225 g diced bacon

Since you're going to cook the meat in fat, it might as well be flavorful fat. Rendered bacon not only delivers flavor from the cure, it also gives the added benefit of the crispy bits of bacon throughout the chili. If you don't have bacon, you could use vegetable or olive oil as a (poor) substitute.

+

GROUND MEAT

2 lb/910 g of beef, pork, turkey, venison (or boar, buffalo, or whatever), or a combination

Cook it in the bacon fat, breaking it up with your spoon until all the pink is gone.

+

SPICES

About ½ cup/60 g spice mix

Spices must be toasted in the rendered fat to bring out
their best flavor and so should be added early in the cooking time,
not at the end. Here's where the skill and personality
factor of making chili show up. Start with a mild chili powder
(almost half the mix) and then add your depth and heat. The
other half is made up of your personal-choice spices, like
the extra smokiness from Spanish paprika, or the richness from
just a touch of unsweetened cocoa powder. You'll figure
out your signature mix over time.

+

VEGETABLES

About 6 cups/680 g
vegetable mix

Use primarily aromatics, such as onions and a generous amount
of garlic. But if you want to bulk up your chili, add sturdier
vegetables that can hold up to the long stewing time. Bell peppers
and carrots, yes; zucchini, no.

+

WET MIX

About 6 cups/
1.4 kg wet mix

Typically beans and tomatoes, including flavorful
liquid such as beer, wine, or stock.

KEVIN DAVIS | STEELHEAD DINER | *Seattle, Washington*

Slow-Braised Pork-Shank Chili

A New Orleans native son, I make chili that is as complex as our legendary Creole one-dish meals.

SERVES

10

LEVEL of DIFFICULTY

WORTH THE EFFORT

REASONABLE

EASY

5 lb/2.3 kg pork shanks, cut osso buco style (approximately six 2-in/5-cm pieces)
Kosher salt

SPICE MIX
¼ cup/30 g New Mexico chile powder
2 tbsp ancho chile powder
2 tbsp chipotle chile powder
2 tbsp ground cumin
1 tsp ground black pepper
1 tsp ground white pepper
1 tsp cayenne pepper

¼ cup/60 ml canola oil
¼ cup/60 ml olive oil
4 garlic cloves, thinly sliced
2 yellow onions, thinly sliced
2 serrano chiles, thinly sliced
2 bay leaves
One 12-oz/360-ml bottle stout beer
Two 14½-oz/415-g cans diced organic tomatoes, with juice
4 qt/3.8 L organic beef stock
1 cup/200 g dried red beans
1 cup/200 g dried pinto beans
1 cup/200 g dried black beans
1 cup/200 g posole (dried hominy)
Tabasco sauce
Leaves from 1 small bunch fresh cilantro, chopped
1 bunch scallions, chopped, plus 4 scallions, sliced
2 tomatoes, diced
Shredded pepper Jack cheese for serving

1. Generously season the pork shanks with salt, then rub all over with a handful of the Spice Mix. Reserve the remaining mix.
2. In a very large, heavy-bottomed pot, heat both oils over medium-high heat. Add the shanks and brown all over, about 4 minutes per side. Transfer to a plate and set aside. Add the garlic to the pot and sauté until just golden, about 2 minutes. Add the onions and chiles and cook, stirring constantly, until tender, about 4 minutes. Add the bay leaves and remaining Spice Mix and cook, stirring constantly to toast the spices, until fragrant, about 3 minutes. Add the beer, canned tomatoes and their juice, and beef stock and stir. Return the pork shanks and any juices on the plate to the pot.
3. Add all the dried beans and the hominy and bring to a boil. Lower the heat to a simmer, cover, and cook, stirring occasionally, until the shanks are very tender, about 3 hours.
4. Remove the shanks from the pot and let cool. Add Tabasco and salt to taste. Keep simmering for a thicker chili; otherwise, remove from the heat and keep warm. When the shanks are cool enough to handle, pull off the meat, discarding the bone, excess fat, and sinew, and return to the pot. Stir in the cilantro and chopped scallions. Return the chili to a simmer and taste, adjusting the seasoning with more salt or Tabasco, if needed.
5. Top with the sliced scallions, diced tomatoes, and cheese before serving.

Posole

When I first moved to Iowa from North Carolina, I hosted a neighborhood dinner for potential restaurant investors and local bigwigs to gather and see if this Midwest newbie could actually cook. There was a lot riding on this meal. I wanted a dish that would show off the bold, fresh flavors I planned to feature at my restaurant. But I also needed to prove myself as a host, so I couldn't get stuck standing over the stove all night. Since it was early spring and not peak growing season—especially in Iowa—I also needed a dish with transitional power. So I made this Mexican chicken *posole*, a way to welcome spring while still offering the comfort of a warming one-pot soup. Ten years later, I'm still here.

Although *posole* is classically prepared with pork shoulder, that day I substituted a great locally raised bird to make the broth, and I used the picked, chopped meat to anchor the dish itself. Here, I call for a convenient good-quality preroasted chicken and store-bought stock (but you can certainly roast your own and make stock from it, if that's up your alley). If you're making the *posole* during the growing season for local chiles, seek out your favorites; for other times, this recipe creates heat by blending two perennial peppers: low notes from canned smoky chipotle and herbal flavors from fresh green jalapeño, available in supermarkets year-round. (Serve your favorite hot sauce at the table to accommodate the masochistic.)

If you can score some of spring's early radishes, their peppery brightness will wake up your palate from winter's root vegetables, and you can also fold the chopped green tops into the soup at the last minute. The hominy is both a Southern tradition and a nod to my Midwestern home, delivering the slightly toasty sweetness of corn when it isn't even in season. You get even more Iowa flavor if you garnish this soup with popcorn. Plus, it floats.

SERVES

6

LEVEL *of* **DIFFICULTY**

WORTH THE EFFORT

REASONABLE

EASY

To warm tortillas, wrap in a stack in a clean kitchen towel and place in a low (200°F/95°C) oven for about 15 minutes before serving.

3 tbsp canola oil

VEGETABLE MIX
1 large yellow onion, chopped
1 large red bell pepper, seeded and chopped
1 poblano chile, seeded and chopped
1 large jalapeño chile, including seeds, chopped
8 garlic cloves, coarsely chopped
1 small bunch kale, stemmed (including tough center spines) and chopped
10 small cremini mushrooms, brushed clean, stemmed, and quartered

SPICE MIX
1 tbsp coarse salt
1 tbsp sugar
1 tbsp orange zest
1 tbsp ground cumin
1 tsp ground coriander
1 tsp dried oregano
¼ tsp ground cinnamon
¼ tsp freshly ground black pepper

1 chipotle chile (from a can of chipotles in adobo sauce), chopped, plus 1 tbsp adobo sauce
Two 14½-oz/415-g cans white hominy, rinsed in a colander under gently running cool water
One 14½-oz/415-g can chopped tomatoes, with juice
5 cups/1.2 L chicken stock
Meat from one 3½-lb/1.6-kg good-quality preroasted chicken, chopped
½ cup/15 g chopped fresh cilantro
6 scallions, chopped
⅓ cup/75 ml fresh lime juice

6 oz/170 g goat cheese, crumbled
2 ripe avocados, pitted, peeled, and sliced
12 small radishes, quartered
Warm flour tortillas for serving*
Hot sauce for serving

1. Heat the canola oil in a large (6-qt/5.7-L) heavy-bottomed pot over medium heat. Add all the Vegetable Mix and cook, stirring occasionally, until the vegetables are softened and the onion begins to color, about 15 minutes.
2. Stir the Spice Mix into the pot, along with the chopped chipotle and adobo sauce. Raise the heat to high and stir until the spices are aromatic, about 1 minute.
3. Add the hominy, the tomatoes and their juice, and the chicken stock. Bring to a boil, then lower the heat to a simmer, cover, and cook, stirring occasionally, until the flavors marry and the soup is thickened, about 30 minutes. Add the chopped chicken, return to a boil, then lower the heat again and simmer for 15 minutes longer.
4. Stir in the cilantro, scallions, and lime juice. Divide the *posole* among soup plates or bowls and garnish with the goat cheese, avocados, and radishes. Serve immediately with warm tortillas. Pass the hot sauce at the table.

Soft-Crab Sandwich

You can tell someone isn't from the Chesapeake region if they say "soft-shell crab." In Baltimore, they're "soft crabs," and we have them in abundance. But that doesn't mean we take them for granted, and I always celebrate their seasonal return with a big sandwich, humble and indulgent at the same time.

Getting soft crabs to market takes a waterman's art and experience. As the water warms up, the dormant crabs get the signal to move; and as they do, they molt their shell, like a snake shedding its skin. That's what creates the window: the waterman must catch and then hold the molting hard crabs in tanks until they lose their shell, and then pack the soft crabs under wet newspaper before the shell hardens again.

Soft crabs must be alive when you buy them. When lifted, the crab should still move a bit. Buy the softest crab you can. To test, *don't* press on the center, as the gills are located under the surface and too much pressure can crush them, killing the crab. Instead, gently pinch the tips of the claws. If they're still soft, that's perfect. The fishmonger will clean the crab in three steps: 1) Snipping off the eyed side with scissors; 2) lifting each side of the soft shell and removing the gills with a paring knife; and 3) turning the crab over to remove the apron (the hingelike tab that resembles a zip top on a can). Cook the crab on the same day you get it cleaned.

The salad I use changes with the season. In early spring, I start with frisée and slivered fennel and radish because that's all there is around. As the weather warms, I layer my sandwich with heartier leaf lettuces, cucumbers, and heirloom tomatoes. But I always go open-face; too much bread can overwhelm the crab—and also, I like to show it off.

SERVES

(multiply for as many as you are willing to make)

LEVEL of DIFFICULTY

WORTH THE EFFORT

REASONABLE

EASY

1 cup/125 g all-purpose flour
1 tbsp cornstarch*
Pinch of ground dry fish pepper**
Coarse salt and freshly ground black
    pepper
1 large or 2 small soft crabs, cleaned
    (see recipe introduction)
3 tbsp unsalted butter***
Tartar sauce for serving
1 thick slice good-quality white
    sandwich bread, lightly buttered
    and toasted until golden in a hot
    skillet or under the broiler
About 1 cup/30 g mixed seasonal salad
    greens, lightly tossed in your favorite
    vinaigrette (such as the one on page 170)
Hot sauce for serving

1. In a shallow bowl or pie tin, combine the flour, cornstarch, fish pepper, a pinch of salt, and a pinch of black pepper. Gently press the crab into the flour mixture, coating both sides and as much of the legs as possible. Shake off the excess. (If there's too much flour, it will fall into the butter during cooking and burn.) Transfer the crab to a rack.
2. In a 10-in/25-cm skillet over medium-high heat, melt the butter until foaming. Add the crab, top-side down, and fry it until golden brown. Carefully turn the crab over and brown the other side.

The total cooking time is 5 to 7 minutes. Transfer to a rack or paper towel to drain briefly and remove excess butter. **3.** To serve, place about 1 tbsp tartar sauce in the center of a plate and top it with the bread. (The tartar sauce will prevent the bread from sliding around.) Spoon more tartar sauce over one edge of the bread, letting some drip onto the plate. Top the bread with the dressed salad and arrange the crab on top of the greens. Pass extra tartar sauce and hot sauce at the side.

✳

Cornstarch brings some extra crunchiness to the simple flour coating.

✳✳

Fish pepper is an heirloom variety that was grown by African Americans in the Chesapeake area in the nineteenth century and is widely prevalent in the region's fish cookery. You can substitute a pinch of cayenne.

✳✳✳

In the restaurant, we use clarified butter, which can get extremely hot without burning. When you are using unsalted butter at home, watch the heat. The crabs need to brown, but the butter mustn't burn.

Cook Like You Mean It

CHRIS JONES

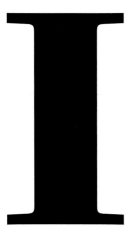

T TOOK A bit for Bryan Voltaggio, the famous young chef with a pig tattooed on his arm, to decide I really was the tragic miracle I'd said I was. We were in the kitchen of his fourth and newest restaurant, Range, in Washington, D.C., pasta and cherry tomatoes and garlic simmering on the stove. A few minutes before, when I was cutting those same cherry tomatoes in half, I told him he was witnessing my first time putting a knife to a vegetable. Not long after, he wondered aloud whether he was being set up as part of some elaborate prank. That's when I mentioned I'd never cracked an egg. "How is that possible?" Voltaggio said. "How are you alive?"

I agreed that it was ridiculous for a thirty-nine-year-old man never to have cracked an egg, that it says something terrible about me as well as modern society that I can survive and in fact grow quite fat without acquiring even the most basic cooking skills, but nevertheless, I had never cracked an egg. Before entering Voltaggio's kitchen, I had possibly prepared the least food of any fully functioning North American adult: one plate of pasta—dried noodles and jarred sauce—just after I'd graduated from Meal Plan University and one serving of Hamburger Helper, with which I'd attempted to court the very good cook who somehow still became my wife. Other than those two barely digestible meals, whenever I have eaten, someone else has made my food for me, either because they love me or because I paid them. Only after Voltaggio watched me nervously crack that first egg did he finally believe me. "Nobody's that good an actor," he said.

Voltaggio comes from a family of cooks and chefs—he finished second to his brother, Michael, on the sixth season of *Top Chef*—and to watch him work in a kitchen is to watch witchcraft, years of experience and observation and fever poured into a cauldron. In some ways, that afternoon at Range confirmed my guiding philosophy: We should do only those things at which we are good. Why would I cook when Bryan Voltaggio cooks? If cooking makes him happy, and eating his food makes me happy, why would I upset that happy order of things? It had never made sense to me, and today it would remain nonsensical but for the fact that after we finished making our pasta, Voltaggio and I made the crab-cake sandwich that changed my life. We didn't just make that sandwich.

We made every last component of that sandwich from its most basic ingredients. We made the soft, hot rolls, washing them with egg and sprinkling them with salt; we made the crab cakes, giant lumps of fresh crab combined with not much else and carefully levered into a pan of clarified butter; we even made the tartar sauce, from Voltaggio's original recipe, that went on top of the crab cakes like a blanket.

Now, here I must confess: While making that tartar sauce, I was consumed by the cynicism of my former self. It took me maybe an hour of work, not including the time I would need at home to find each of its fourteen ingredients. It required making grapeseed oil shimmer in the pan but not smoke—canola oil would smell like rotting fish, Voltaggio said, the sort of wisdom that seems impossible for me to own—and sweating diced celery, fennel, and onions, but not browning them. Alternatively, I could go out and buy a jar of tartar sauce in about six seconds. But then I finished Voltaggio's recipe, and I tasted it, and I understood. It wasn't some small fraction better than factory-born tartar sauce. It was better by orders of magnitude, turning something incidental into something essential. I can't recall eating any single tartar sauce in my life except for that one. Then we put it on the sandwich, and then we ate the sandwich, and holy sweet Mary mother of baby Jesus, it was the best sandwich I have ever eaten. It was the sandwich I had been dreaming about my whole life put suddenly where it belonged, in my open, groaning mouth.

What Voltaggio taught me, more than anything else, is that there is no particular magic in that trick. He refuses to call food *art*, or cooking *artistry*. That makes it sound more precious and inaccessible than it is. All good cooking requires, at its foundation, is generosity. Every decent meal I have eaten I have enjoyed because someone else had a big enough heart to make it.

I always thought of my refusal to cook as a selfless act: I was sparing the world my barbarism. In reality, learning how to make delicious whole food requires a capacity for goodness that I wish I didn't have to work so hard to possess. Yes, at some level, that crab-cake sandwich was just a sandwich, just caloric energy presented in a photogenic shape. But it was also this beautiful expression of care, this tender, charitable agreement that Bryan Voltaggio had made to teach me how to do some tiny fraction of what he does and to help me feel as though I could do more of it. I will make those crab-cake sandwiches again and again, partly because I couldn't live with the idea of never eating another one, but mostly because it will allow me to give something meaningful, my time and my effort, my attention and my education, to the people who remind me not only how I am alive but also why.

Maryland Crab-Cake Sandwiches

Cooking is not an art. Cooking is generosity. Crab-cake sandwiches are proof of that.

SERVES

6

LEVEL *of*
DIFFICULTY

WORTH
THE EFFORT

REASONABLE

EASY

You can buy prepared clarified butter (usually packaged as ghee) or make it yourself: For about 1 cup/250 ml, in a small saucepan, slowly melt 1½ cups/330 g unsalted butter. When it starts bubbling, remove from the heat. Spoon off the white milk solids from the surface and discard. Pour the golden yellow layer of clarified butter into a container—this is what you will cook with. Discard the solids remaining on the bottom.

7 tbsp/100 g mayonnaise, preferably
    Duke's (Hellmann's, if you live up north)
1 tbsp Old Bay seasoning
2½ tsp Worcestershire sauce
2½ tsp Dijon mustard
3¾ tsp fresh lemon juice
2 large eggs
4 scallions, minced
6 drops Tabasco sauce
½ tsp fine sea salt
2 lb/910 g jumbo lump crabmeat,
    picked over for shell fragments
1 cup/110 g cracker meal
1 cup/250 ml clarified butter*
6 puffy buns, split, toasted, and buttered
Tartar sauce for serving

1. In a medium bowl, combine the mayonnaise, Old Bay, Worcestershire, mustard, lemon juice, eggs, scallions, Tabasco, and salt. Whisk until thoroughly blended. Add the crabmeat one-third at a time, folding in gently with a spatula to be sure the crab does not get broken up.

2. Generously coat the bottom of a baking dish with about ½ cup/55 g of the cracker meal. Using a large spoon or an ice-cream scoop, divide the crabmeat mixture into six or eight individual cakes. Place each crab cake in the cracker meal in the dish and then dust with the remaining cracker meal, coating all sides.

3. In a large skillet over medium heat, slowly heat the clarified butter to 325°F/165°C. Use a deep-frying thermometer—or stick the end of a chopstick into the butter; when it gives off a steady stream of bubbles, you're at the correct temperature.

4. Using a slotted metal or other high-heat-resistant spatula, place one crab cake at a time into the butter, leaving about ½ in/12 mm between them so they brown evenly. Cook, turning once carefully, until golden brown, about 6 minutes per side. Transfer to a wire rack or paper towels to rest. (If you need to cook in multiple batches, set your oven at the lowest temperature and place a wire rack set on a baking sheet inside, to hold each batch of crab cakes as they are finished.) Let the cakes rest for at least 1 minute after they're done.

5. Transfer the cakes to the buttered buns and top with tartar sauce to serve.

| EVAN MALLETT | BLACK TRUMPET | *Portsmouth, New Hampshire* |

Fried Fish Sandwiches

My wife's love of fish sandwiches runs deep: Canadian blood flows thick in her veins, and her childhood on Cape Cod forged a discerning palate. Most attempts don't live up to her lofty expectations. In creating the ultimate at-home fishwich for summer, those expectations were my guide. The greatest challenge was selecting the right fish. Haddock is mild and delicate but cod has large, sturdy flakes and a more distinct flavor, so that's my first choice. As for the buns: bakery fresh if you can, supermarket if you must. Another subject my wife feels strongly about: proper accoutrements. You need pickles, for one thing. And coleslaw, keeping in mind that most homemade slaws taste better than the mayo-drenched deli variety. A bag of chips is good—I recommend the Route 11 dill-pickle potato chips—unless you're making french fries, which you can, using preblanched fries in the leftover oil . . . but that's another undertaking altogether. The fact is, you could do without any of that as long as you have plenty of cold beer.

SERVES

10

LEVEL *of* **DIFFICULTY**

WORTH THE EFFORT

REASONABLE

EASY

2 cups/255 g all-purpose flour
2 tsp sea salt
½ tsp freshly ground black pepper
½ tsp paprika
½ tsp celery salt
½ tsp ground coriander
2 tsp baking soda
2 cups/480 ml cold beer*
4 cups/960 ml peanut oil
Ten 3-oz/85-g thin pieces of cod or
    haddock fillet,** skin removed
    if necessary, patted dry
10 puffy buns, split, smeared with
    softened butter, and toasted
    (butter-side down) in a hot skillet

Beer batter makes the best crust. We like Pabst Blue Ribbon (yep) and English pale ale. The ale has better flavor and texture, but the PBR crust was light and crispy and will do any day.

Hake, pollock, and cusk may be substituted for the halibut.

1. Preheat the oven to 250°F/120°C.
2. In a large bowl, whisk together the flour, sea salt, pepper, paprika, celery salt, coriander, and baking soda. Gradually whisk in the beer. (The batter should be similar to pancake batter in thickness.) Set aside. →

3. Heat the oil in a 10-in/25-cm cast-iron skillet with tall sides. (The oil should be about 1 in/2.5 cm deep.) When it reaches 275°F/135°C (use a candy or deep-frying thermometer), lower the heat to a maintain a simmer. (A drop of batter will float to the top and fizzle without burning.)

4. Working with one fillet at a time, insert a fork or two-tined meat fork into the top one-third of the fish (so most of it is hanging down) and gently swirl it in the batter to coat completely. Then place—don't drop—it in the oil. Repeat to add more fillets. (Cook the fish in two or three batches. Overcrowding the pan will lower the oil temperature and cause the batter to fall off the fish and burn to the bottom of the pan.)

5. If the fish is not completely submerged in oil, use tongs to flip after 30 seconds, and flip again after 1 minute. Fry the fish until the coating is the color of lightly stained oak, about 4 minutes total. As they come out of the pan, transfer to a brown paper bag flattened on the countertop or a wire rack and let rest for a minute—the steam inside the crust will continue to cook the fish.

6. When the first batch of fish has gone in the frying pan, put the split, toasted buns flat-side down on two large baking sheets and put them in the oven to warm. There should be no need to reheat the first batch of fish by the time the last batch is done, but if the process goes slowly, you can warm the fish in the oven with the buns. The fish stays pretty hot inside its thermal coat, so it can stand to be at room temp for about 5 minutes before you need to think about popping it into the oven.

7. To serve, place a warm buttered bun on each plate. Slide a fried fish fillet on top of each, and close up the sandwiches.

In Praise of the 5-Gallon Igloo Cooler

DAVID WONDRICH

MANAGING A BACKYARD full of tipsy friends is one of the great underappreciated adult skills. It's easy to get people stinking drunk, if they're the drinking kind. Three rounds of real margaritas—the kind that's just good tequila, fresh lime juice, and Cointreau—before the food comes out and you might as well be entertaining so many ring-tailed lemurs for all the sense you'll get out of your guests. It's also easy to under-ethanolize them: Just make free, but not too free, with the pinot grigio or light beer and watch the awkward pauses and covert glances at timepieces multiply.

For getting it just right, we know of nothing more effective than the 5-gallon Igloo cooler full of old-school punch. The vessel might not be elegant, but it keeps the cold in and the flies out, and after a couple cups of this punch—which bears as much resemblance to the swill usually dished out under its name as the gin martini does to the chocotini—nobody will give a damn what it's being served from. Not too strong, not too sweet, plenty refreshing, and tasting just boozy enough to remind you to go easy, it has the additional advantage of slowly getting weaker as the ice melts— in case you forget the go-easy part.

PUNCH

Put your kids to work juicing lemons. You'll need **6 CUPS/ 1.4 L STRAINED LEMON JUICE**, which should be about 36 lemons' worth. Stir **6 CUPS/ 1.2 KG SUPERFINE SUGAR** into the lemon juice until it dissolves and pour this into the cooler. Add **FOUR 750-ML BOTTLES COGNAC** (it doesn't have to be fancy) and **THREE 750-ML BOTTLES DARK, FUNKY RUM** (Pusser's works well here, or—even better— two bottles Gosling's and one Wray & Nephew White Overproof). Add **7 QT/6.6 L WATER**. Grate in 1½ **WHOLE NUTMEGS** and stir. Fill the cooler the rest of the way with **ICE** and put the top on. At this point, we like to tape a label on the front so everyone knows what they're getting into. It's always nice to christen your punch, preferably after some local geographic feature. Serve in cups no larger than 4 to 6 oz/ 120 to 180 ml. **THIS MAKES ABOUT 125 SERVINGS OF 4 OZ/120 ML EACH.**

Fried Bologna Sandwiches with Pickled Slaw

Although I came from a food-loving family and grew up to be a chef, my dad didn't pass down any soufflé recipes. For him, it was all about the sandwich, and he taught me to pay attention to every part. That means buying meats and cheeses sliced to order from the deli and using good-quality bakery bread, light but sturdy, so it won't get soggy when it comes in contact with the filling. You also want to slice the loaf yourself so that you can balance the ratio of the filling to the bread—let's say 30 percent filling to 35 percent bread on either side. The last consideration is the most important: You must offset the richness of the meat with some acidity, whether pickles, slaw, or, in the case of this ultra-rich bologna, the double whammy of pickled slaw. Because whether it's made by the dad or the son, a good sandwich is about relationships.

SERVES

4

LEVEL *of*
DIFFICULTY

WORTH
THE EFFORT

REASONABLE

EASY

SLAW
½ head napa cabbage, shredded
½ garlic clove, minced
½ small red onion, thinly sliced
½ jalapeño chile, seeded and minced
½ cup chopped sweet hot pickles
   (available in jars), drained
3 tbsp Champagne vinegar
1 tbsp Worcestershire sauce
1 tbsp Dijon mustard
1 tbsp spicy brown mustard
2 tbsp mayonnaise
1 tbsp sugar
1½ tsp salt

Olive oil for frying
8 pieces thick-sliced bologna
   (not prepackaged)
8 pieces good-quality white bread

1. TO MAKE THE SLAW:
In a large bowl, toss together the cabbage, garlic, onion, jalapeño, and pickles. In a small bowl, whisk together the vinegar, Worcestershire, both mustards, mayonnaise, sugar, and salt. Pour over the cabbage mixture and stir to coat thoroughly. Refrigerate for 1 hour.
2. Preheat a large sauté pan over medium-high heat. When the pan is hot, add just enough olive oil to film the bottom of the pan. Add the bologna in a single layer, working in batches if necessary (if the pan is too crowded, the meat will steam, not brown). Cook the bologna until browned on both sides, about 1 minute per side, then transfer to a plate.
3. Lay out 4 pieces of the bread. Place 2 slices of bologna on each slice and top with one-fourth of the slaw. Top with the other pieces of bread and press down lightly. Cut in half and dive in.

EXTREMELY
EASY
RECIPE

MOCK CHEESESTEAK

Split 2 **BAGUETTES** open lengthwise—but don't separate the halves—and lay them cut-side up on sheet pans (probably one per pan). Preheat the oven to 350°F/165°C. In a big saucepan, bring **2 QT/ 2 L BEEF STOCK** to a simmer. Using tongs and working with only a few slices at a time, dip **2 LB/910 G THIN-SLICED GOOD- QUALITY DELI ROAST BEEF** into the stock and gently swirl just long enough to warm it. Layer the wet beef across the bottom halves of the baguettes, top with **SLICED CHEESE (PROVOLONE, MUENSTER, OR EVEN PEPPER JACK),** and toast in the oven until the cheese melts, about 3 minutes. Sprinkle each sandwich with some **PICKLED HOT PEPPERS** and close with the top halves of the baguettes. Cut each baguette into four sections. Eat. Repeat until the game is over. **SERVES 4.**

Pulled Pork Sandwiches

It's not just the flavors that make a dish but the layering of textures. I love pulled pork because of the contrast between the crispy exterior and the tender, almost-melting inside. You start with a pork "butt" (actually a pig's shoulder), a cheap but flavorful cut with a good amount of fat that renders out during the long, slow cooking and bastes the meat to give it a caramelized crust.

A pulled pork sandwich should be messy; that makes it perfect summer-by-the-pool food at my house. I recently added an outdoor party kitchen with a rotisserie, and I roast all kinds of things, including birds and prime ribs. It works great for pork butt, too. Or if you have a smoker, this is also an awesome piece of meat to smoke. (Just follow the same recipe using the smoker instead of the oven.)

This is a dish you can make a day ahead with no hassle; just reheat it with some of your favorite barbecue sauce and serve it on plain soft white rolls. (You don't want a real serious roll that is going to interfere with the flavor of the meat.) Because it can even be served at room temperature, I bring this to our tailgates before 49ers games. A little extra barbecue sauce or hot sauce and maybe some mustard, and you're all set. Accompany with classic barbecue side dishes like Bourbon Baked Beans (page 188).

SERVES

6

LEVEL of DIFFICULTY

WORTH THE EFFORT

REASONABLE

EASY

¼ cup/50 g lightly packed dark
    brown sugar
2 tbsp kosher or coarse salt
2 tbsp paprika
1 tbsp freshly ground black pepper
½ tbsp ground coriander
½ tsp dry mustard
½ tsp onion powder
One 3-lb/1.4-kg boneless pork butt*
1½ cups/360 ml apple juice
½ cup/120 ml water
6 to 8 plain soft white rolls, split →

You can buy bone-in or boneless pork butts. Both have their benefits: Cooking bone-in will contribute some flavor (and increase the cooking time slightly). But if you have your butcher take out the bone, you can rub the spice mix into the incisions where the bone was removed—a great way to get the flavor deep inside the meat.

1. In a small bowl, stir together the brown sugar, salt, paprika, pepper, coriander, dry mustard, and onion powder. Rub the spice mixture all over the pork. Cover and let sit in the refrigerator for as long as you have time for, preferably at least 1 hour or up to overnight.

2. Preheat the oven to 300°F/150°C.

3. Place the pork on a rack fitted inside a roasting pan. (The rack should be high enough so the entire spiced butt is sitting above the cooking liquid.) Pour in the apple juice and water, cover the pan tightly with aluminum foil, and slow-roast for 5 hours. Remove the foil and continue roasting until the pork is browned outside and the meat is very tender, basically falling apart, about 30 minutes longer.

4. Remove the pork from the oven, transfer to a large platter, and let rest for about 10 minutes. While still warm, shred the pork into small pieces using two forks or ten fingers. Transfer to a bowl for serving, or cover and refrigerate for up to 2 days. (To reheat, just transfer to a shallow baking dish, bring to room temperature, and place in a preheated 350°F/180°C oven for 15 minutes.)

5. Place a roll on each plate and pile the shredded pork into the rolls to serve.

TIP

We use a roasting pan that isn't much bigger than the meat itself, so the drippings don't spread out and burn. If the pan drippings aren't burned, spoon off the fat and mix the drippings back into the pulled pork; that will make it even more moist and flavorful.

Mustard-and-Beer-Braised Sausages

New Orleans chef Donald Link's German heritage shines through in this artery-displeasing Cajun combination of sausage, sauerkraut, and a beer. Sound like enough flavor for you? Not for the man behind Cochon, who adds apples to nudge the brine outta the 'kraut and poblano chiles to bring up the heat. Best way to get all the ingredients to play nice? Cook 'em down in Louisiana-brewed Abita beer, which is good enough to track down a case of in case you're rooting for the Saints in the Super Bowl. Which Link most certainly is: "This dish is as easy to prepare as it is to eat," he says. "I want to be watching the game without any distractions."

SERVES

12

LEVEL *of* DIFFICULTY

WORTH THE EFFORT

REASONABLE

EASY

3 lb/1.4 kg pork sausages (the good stuff, from a butcher)
2 tbsp vegetable oil
2 yellow onions, sliced
2 poblano chiles, seeded and sliced
6 cups/1.4 kg sauerkraut
2 apples, preferably Granny Smith or Golden Delicious, peeled, cored, and cut into ½-in/12-mm dice
½ cup/120 g whole-grain mustard
One 16-oz/480-ml bottle Abita Amber beer

1. In your heaviest skillet, sear the sausages in the oil over medium heat until they begin to brown, about 5 minutes.
2. Add the onions and chiles and keep cooking for about 3 minutes more, or until the vegetables soften.
3. Add the sauerkraut, apples, and mustard and stir to mix. Slowly pour in the beer. Simmer for 10 minutes, tops, before serving—you're really just looking for the beer to reduce by at least two-thirds. And then you're looking to drink one.

Three Variations on the Burger

FRANCINE MAROUKIAN

WHEN I WAS a kid, my father's grilling method had a theatrical lights-camera-action quality. First, he would pile briquettes into a loose, lumpy pyramid and douse it with lighter fluid. Then, from a safe distance of several feet, he would fire a match onto the pile, dramatically commanding, "Stand back!"

A space-age later, grilling has changed a whole lot since Sunday in the yard with Dad. The charcoal briquettes that made food taste as if it had been cooked on the grille of my dad's DeSoto have given way to natural hardwood charcoal and wood chips that lend a distinct smokiness to your grilled food; the wobbly Weber grills on tinny tripods that we used to dust off as warm weather approached have morphed into sleek stainless-steel outdoor ranges suitable for year-round use.

Unfortunately, the trend has spawned the grill fanatic, the kind of guy with money to burn who corners me at a cocktail party to explain in excruciating detail how he's perfected the art of the backyard soufflé or to annotate his latest barbecue accomplishments involving guava-soy marinade, foie gras, and strategically balanced lemongrass.

I'm always tempted to stop such conversations by blurting out, "Not in my backyard!" Usually, though, I just confess my nostalgia for simple backyard barbecues: a bunch of guys standing around poking at meat with a fork while women set the table and children run amok.

I don't require much in the way of exotica on the grill, either. A juicy burger with slightly charred edges on a lightly toasted roll is all it takes to guarantee that I'll be a grateful guest.

A good grilled burger starts with freshly ground meat. Ask your butcher to grind the meat only once (coarsely), then add a few simple ingredients to impart flavor and keep the meat moist. (This is particularly important when you are cooking ground lean meat past medium-rare.) And remember: No matter how thick the burger is, pressing down on it with a spatula will *not* speed up the cooking process—you'll just lose flavorful juices. That's all you need to know to become the best kind of grill guy, the kind who can provide a fabulous meal without having to explain how it was done.

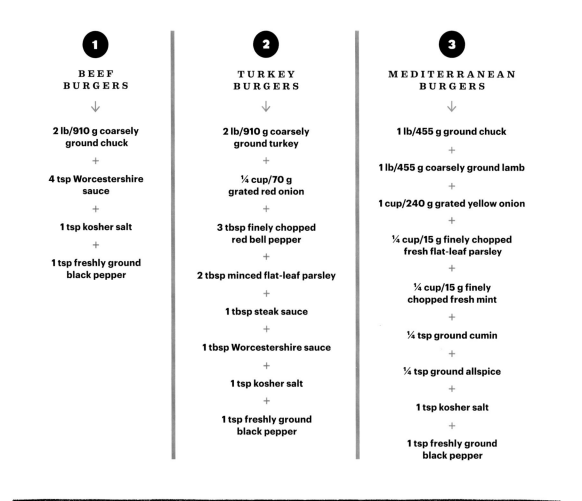

1

BEEF BURGERS

↓

2 lb/910 g coarsely ground chuck

+

4 tsp Worcestershire sauce

+

1 tsp kosher salt

+

1 tsp freshly ground black pepper

2

TURKEY BURGERS

↓

2 lb/910 g coarsely ground turkey

+

¼ cup/70 g grated red onion

+

3 tbsp finely chopped red bell pepper

+

2 tbsp minced flat-leaf parsley

+

1 tbsp steak sauce

+

1 tbsp Worcestershire sauce

+

1 tsp kosher salt

+

1 tsp freshly ground black pepper

3

MEDITERRANEAN BURGERS

↓

1 lb/455 g ground chuck

+

1 lb/455 g coarsely ground lamb

+

1 cup/240 g grated yellow onion

+

¼ cup/15 g finely chopped fresh flat-leaf parsley

+

¼ cup/15 g finely chopped fresh mint

+

¼ tsp ground cumin

+

¼ tsp ground allspice

+

1 tsp kosher salt

+

1 tsp freshly ground black pepper

1. Build a hot fire in a charcoal grill or preheat a gas grill to high.

2. Choose your Burger. Combine the ingredients in a large bowl and mix gently. Do not overmix. Shape into four patties—form the burgers loosely or they will dry out while cooking.

3. Arrange the burgers on the grill rack and cook for 3 to 4 minutes on the first side, then 2 to 3 minutes on the flip side for rare; add another minute or so per side for medium-rare. When grilling burgers past this point, you are treading the fine line between burgers and pet rocks. For turkey burgers, which need to be thoroughly cooked, and for other burgers you for some reason need well-done, check often after 9 or 10 minutes total cooking time. **SERVES 4 WITH 8-OZ/225-G BURGERS**

BRIAN BISTRONG | **BOTTEGA** | *Yountville, California*

St. Louis Pork Ribs

With all their talk of fruitwoods versus hardwoods, secret dry-rub ingredients, and brining formulas, barbecue aficionados (bless them) have made rib cookery into something more complicated than it needs to be. This technique produces moist, melt-off-the-bone spareribs that are delicious and require minimal effort. They're as easy to serve as they are to prepare—no knives, no forks, just plenty of napkins. Finish them off in your oven's broiler or an outdoor grill. Either way, they don't require too much attention—a good thing, since you've probably got a game to watch.

SERVES

4

LEVEL *of* **DIFFICULTY**

WORTH THE EFFORT
REASONABLE
EASY

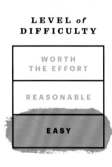

For store-bought barbecue sauce, try Baby Jake's.

2 racks fresh St. Louis pork ribs
1 bay leaf
2 sprigs fresh thyme
2 tbsp kosher salt
2 tbsp freshly ground black pepper
3 qt/2.8 L chicken stock
Barbecue sauce (as much sauce as you like)*

1. Cut the rib racks in half so they fit into a large pot or Dutch oven. Place the ribs in the pot and add the bay leaf, thyme, salt, pepper, and chicken stock. Bring to a boil over medium-high heat, then lower the heat to maintain a gentle simmer. Simmer until very tender but not falling apart, 1 to 2 hours. (If the simmering broth starts to boil, just add a little cold water to the pot.) Using tongs, transfer the ribs to a platter and let cool.

2. Build a medium-hot fire in a charcoal grill or preheat a gas grill to medium, or preheat the broiler.
3. Using a pastry brush, coat the ribs all over with barbecue sauce. Arrange the ribs on the grill rack or broiler pan and grill or broil, turning once, until the barbecue sauce begins to blister and the meat becomes slightly charred, 5 or 6 minutes per side. Cut the ribs into sections along the bone, pile onto a serving platter or individual plates, and serve immediately with a fistful of napkins.

Roaster Chicken Wings

This highly seasoned buttermilk marinade may be a departure from your tried-and-true wing recipe, but fans of Scampo in Boston swear by it. I suggest you buy the biggest, meatiest wings you can find and marinate them overnight. (We're dealing with some pretty assertive spices here, so the wings are going to pick up lots of flavor.) Make sure to keep the cooking oil at a steady 325°F/165°C to lock all that flavor into a golden, crunchy skin. If you want to make these wings even tastier, use a blend of cooking oils—don't be afraid to add some lard, butter, even Crisco. Each fat will bring something new to the dish.

SERVES

LEVEL *of* **DIFFICULTY**

WORTH THE EFFORT

REASONABLE

EASY

MARINADE
1 qt/960 ml buttermilk
1 yellow onion, diced
3 stalks celery, with leaves, thinly sliced
2 tbsp celery seed
2 tbsp celery salt
2 tbsp Madras curry powder
1 tbsp ground coriander
1 tbsp ground cumin
1 tbsp cayenne pepper
1 tbsp kosher salt
1 tsp freshly ground black pepper
Juice and zest of 1 lemon

3 lb/1.4 kg chicken wings, tips snipped off and split at the "elbow"
2 qt/2 L peanut oil
3 cups/380 g unbleached all-purpose flour
3 tbsp kosher salt
2 tbsp freshly ground black pepper
1 tbsp cayenne pepper
Hot sauce for serving

1. TO MAKE THE MARINADE: In a bowl large enough to accommodate the chicken wings, whisk together all of the marinade ingredients. Let stand at room temperature for 15 to 20 minutes.

2. Add the chicken wings to the marinade and turn to coat thoroughly. Cover and let marinate in the refrigerator overnight.

3. Pour the peanut oil into a Dutch oven or other heavy-bottomed pot, or a deep fryer. Heat the oil to 325°F/165°C on a deep-frying or candy thermometer.

4. In a shallow bowl, whisk together the flour, salt, pepper, and cayenne. Remove the chicken wings from the marinade and drain them. Dredge the chicken wings in the flour mixture, making sure that the wings are well coated on all sides. Shake the excess flour from the wings and carefully add five or six to the hot oil; do not crowd the pot. Cook until golden brown, about 10 minutes. Using tongs, a slotted spoon, or a skimmer, transfer to paper towels to drain. Repeat to fry all the wings, making sure to let the oil return to 325°F/165°C between batches.

5. When all the wings are fried, pile them on a platter and serve immediately with your favorite hot sauce.

Dinner

Mushroom Lasagna

After twenty years submerged in New York's changing restaurant scene, I know one thing for sure: The City that Never Sleeps also can't keep its mouth shut. It's not just the volume. Crowds and cramped tables guarantee that by the end of any evening, I will know too much about something I shouldn't know at all.

Sometimes, in order to have a good meal and conversation all my own, it's easier to just stay home and cook. Especially on weekends. Although it may not compete with the nightlife most out-of-towners imagine when they think of New York, I am able to lure people over by mentioning a quiet evening. Then I promise to coddle them with something simple, something homey—something with a lot of melted cheese.

You'd be surprised at how effective my offer is during the late fall, when Sunday nights take on that weird, school-tomorrow sadness, no matter how old you are. Everyone seems to want a little culinary reassurance, the kind of food you don't have to figure out how to eat. I try to make something that tastes familiar without being boring, like this porcini-laced lasagna, an elevated version of that old cafeteria classic. We pass the plates around in silent agreement: It's not really comfort food unless you're comfortable.

SERVES

8

LEVEL *of* DIFFICULTY

WORTH THE EFFORT

REASONABLE

EASY

Keep the mushroom types separate from one another.

4 oz/115 g dried porcini mushrooms*
2 cups/480 ml boiling water
4 cups/960 ml tomato sauce
8 oz/230 g dried lasagna noodles
　　or no-boil noodles
3 tbsp olive oil
1½ lb/680 g portobello mushrooms,*
　　brushed clean and stemmed,
　　cut into ½-in/12-mm dice
½ lb/230 g large white mushrooms,*
　　brushed clean and stemmed,
　　thinly sliced
Kosher salt and freshly ground
　　black pepper
1½ cups/125 g freshly grated
　　Parmigiano-Reggiano cheese
¼ cup/10 g finely chopped fresh
　　flat-leaf parsley
1 cup/245 g ricotta cheese
1 cup/240 ml heavy cream

1. Put the porcinis in a heatproof bowl and slowly pour the boiling water over them. Let the mushrooms soak until softened, at least 30 minutes. Using a slotted spoon, transfer the porcinis to a cutting board. Strain the soaking liquid through a double thickness of cheesecloth into a saucepan. You should have about ½ cup/120 ml. Bring to a gentle boil over medium heat and cook until reduced to about ¼ cup/60 ml. Stir into the tomato sauce and set aside. Finely chop the porcinis and set aside.

2. To cook the noodles (if you are using no-boil noodles, skip this step), bring a large pot of abundantly salted water to a boil. Meanwhile, set up a large bowl of ice water, and line a baking pan with clean, dampened kitchen towels. Dampen two more kitchen towels and set aside. Add the lasagna noodles, three or four at a time, to the boiling water and cook until al dente. Using a slotted spoon or a mesh spider (tongs will tear the noodles), immediately transfer the noodles to the bowl of ice water to stop the cooking process, then remove, drain thoroughly, and spread on the kitchen towels. Repeat, putting a dampened towel between each layer of noodles.

3. In a large sauté pan, heat the olive oil over medium heat until hot but not smoking (a drop of water should sizzle immediately upon contact). Sauté the portobello mushrooms in small batches (do not crowd the pan), stirring until golden brown, 5 to 7 minutes per batch, transferring each batch to a large bowl when it's done. Use the same technique to cook the white mushrooms, then add them to the bowl. Stir in the porcini. Season with salt and pepper and toss to combine; set aside to cool.

4. Preheat the oven to 350°F/180°C. Lightly oil a 9-by-13-in/23-by-33-cm ovenproof baking dish. In a small bowl, mix 2 tbsp of the Parmigiano with 1 tbsp of the parsley. In another bowl, combine the ricotta with the cream; mix ¼ cup/60 ml of the tomato sauce with one-quarter of the ricotta mixture (reserving the rest) and set aside.

5. Arrange one layer of noodles, touching but not overlapping, on the bottom of the prepared baking dish. Cover the noodles with about one-third each of the mushrooms, sauce, ricotta mixture, and Parmigiano-parsley mixture. Top with a few grinds of black pepper. Add two more layers, then top with a final layer of noodles. Spread the reserved sauce and ricotta mixture over the top, then sprinkle with the remaining Parmigiano and parsley.

6. Cover the dish tightly with aluminum foil and bake until the edges are bubbling, 35 minutes. Remove the foil and bake until the top is lightly browned, 10 to 15 minutes longer. Let rest for 10 to 15 minutes, then cut into big squares to serve.

To serve 16, make a second pan, but don't double the recipe from the outset; combine the filling for each lasagna in separate bowls. There isn't a great deal of ricotta, so if the ratio and portions aren't exactly right, the lasagna noodles won't be properly supported, impacting cooking time and possibly turning a portion into a sliding pile of noodles.

Baked Ditalini with Spicy Sausage, Broccoli Rabe, and White Beans

Whether the crowd gathers at my place or someone else's, I'm always the designated pasta guy. You have to be smart about cooking pasta for a crowd: the more people you cook for, the shorter the pasta should be. Spaghetti might work for a few people, but when you're feeding an army, you need something more manageable. Here I use ditalini, a small, plain tube, because more ornate shapes don't cook as evenly. Also, since the sausage is one of the stars in this dish—it flavors everything during the cooking process—buy good quality. Once assembled, you can either bake the dish right away or wait until guests arrive. Forty minutes later, you're a hero.

SERVES

LEVEL *of* DIFFICULTY

WORTH THE EFFORT

REASONABLE

EASY

6 tbsp/90 ml extra-virgin olive oil
2 garlic cloves, thinly sliced
4 bunches broccoli rabe, florets and leaves chopped into large pieces, stems chopped into small, thin pieces
6 large pinches of kosher salt
6 large pinches of freshly ground black pepper
6 large pinches of red pepper flakes
3 tbsp chopped fresh rosemary
Two 28-oz/794-g cans crushed San Marzano tomatoes (if you have whole tomatoes, purée them in a blender)

3 lb/1.4 kg ditalini pasta or other small, plain shape
2 lb/910 g hot Italian sausage, removed from casings and crumbled
5 cups/1.3 kg cooked white beans, drained
2 qt/2 L chicken or vegetable stock
4 cups/460 g freshly grated Parmigiano-Reggiano cheese
1½ cups/170 g seasoned bread crumbs →

1. Preheat the oven to 375°F/190°C. Bring a large pot of salted water to a boil.

2. While the water is heating, place two deep 12-in/30.5-cm skillets over high heat. Place 3 tbsp of the oil and 1 sliced garlic clove in each pan and cook until the garlic turns golden brown, about 2 minutes. Add half of the broccoli rabe to each pan, sautéing until wilted, about 3 minutes. (The broccoli rabe will start out as a mountain but deflate as it cooks. Use tongs to rotate it as the leaves wilt.) To each pan, add half of the salt, pepper, red pepper flakes, and rosemary and toss to combine. Add 1 can of tomatoes to each pan and cook until the sauce thickens slightly, 8 to 10 minutes.

3. The pasta water should be boiling by now, so drop in the ditalini and cook for 5 minutes. (The pasta must be undercooked, as it will finish in the oven.)

4. While the pasta is cooking, divide the sausage in half and add one portion to each pan, stirring to heat and incorporate it, about 2 minutes. (You're not trying to cook it through at this point.) Add half of the beans to each pan, stir to combine, and remove from the heat.

5. Once the pasta has cooked for 5 minutes, drain it in a colander. Pour both pans of sauce into the warm big pasta pot, then add the pasta back in and mix thoroughly. Although the pasta should still be hard, taste and adjust the seasoning. Place over low heat. Add the stock to the pot a little at a time, bringing it to a simmer, until the pasta mixture is a bit soupy, but not swimming. (If assembling ahead of time, add more stock to keep the pasta moist. The longer it sits before baking, the more liquid the pasta will absorb.) Remove from the heat and stir in 1 cup/115 g of the Parmigiano.

6. Transfer the pasta mixture to two baking dishes (9-by-13-in/23-by-33-cm or 11-by-14-in/28-by-35.5-cm, or even one of each). In a bowl, mix the remaining 3 cups/345 g Parmigiano with the bread crumbs and sprinkle liberally and evenly over the top of each dish. (Do not stir into the pasta.)

7. Bake until the tops are golden and bubbling slightly around the edges, about 30 minutes. (If the top of the pasta does not brown, turn the oven to broil for a few minutes before removing the pans from the oven.) Let rest for about 10 minutes, then scoop generously into pasta bowls and serve immediately.

HOW TO

BE A HOST

*Whether you're on the offering or accepting end of an invitation,
entertaining is a relationship between a host and his guests, a connection made
better when both parties understand their particular roles.*

↓

1

SET THE STAGE

Whatever the style—e-vite,
low-tech traditional printed, or
telephone—the most important
aspect of an invitation is clarity:
Tell guests *who* is inviting them
where and *when*, and exactly
what to expect: Will there
be a buffet supper? Super Bowl
chili and beer? A barbecue?
This helps set the party tone
and gives people a sense of
what to wear. In order to help
convey the mood, you can also
explain *why* you're giving
a party (especially when there
is a birthday or anniversary
involved) and most certainly
use the invitation to indicate
anything special guests should
do, like bring a bottle, don
a costume, or keep a secret.

2

BE READY

Organize your party plan, make a work list, and give yourself
plenty of time to finish before guests arrive. A harried host is the
antithesis of hospitality—fussing and making adjustments
after guests arrive gives people an uncomfortable glimpse into
the machinery that sets your party in motion.

3

YOU'RE ONLY AS GOOD AS YOUR GUESTS

A host's most significant contribution to a party's success is
assembling a dynamic guest list. Delicious food and just the
right music won't matter if you don't have a lively mix of people.
The worst common denominator for any guest list is a sense
of obligation (and don't kid yourself, guests can feel it). You'll be
a better host (and have a better time) if you draw on people from
different parts of your world, combining business associates,
social acquaintances, and "pay-backs" with close friends you
can count on to be irresistibly charming.

4

PLAN A CROWD-PLEASING MENU

Planning a menu around the likes and dislikes of guests
will make entertaining impossible: there won't be anything
left to serve. Considerate menu planning means selecting
dishes that almost everyone can enjoy (easy on the exotica)
and are easy to handle (no bones at buffets). There's
nothing wrong with falling back on standards like a great
roast with mashed potatoes or an old-school stew. There's
a reason these dishes are called "crowd-pleasers," and
there's certainly nothing wrong with that.

5

SAY HELLO AND
THEN SAY GOOD-BYE

Greeting guests at the door when they
arrive is the warmest welcome a host
can offer. But letting them know it's
time to leave is equally important—and
flickering the lights isn't the way to go.
Instead, pass a tray of chocolates
and offer coffee for the road, thanking
your guests for coming.

NICK ANDERER | **MAIALINO** | *New York, New York*

Pork Bolognese

Bolognese is the essential meat sauce of Emilia-Romagna's rich food culture, and nothing stops the people of that region from eating it year-round. But it's also a sensible between-seasons dish while we wait for the markets to fill with spring's early greens. A good Bolognese is vibrant enough to wake us from the hibernating foods of winter and satisfying enough to bridge that unpredictable gap when the weather isn't quite as warm as we think it is.

As complex as the flavor is, this Bolognese is a straightforward, short-simmered sauce. The most important moment comes in cooking the pasta itself, a single step that can make the dish great or just okay. Executing this step properly will allow the spaghetti's starch to flow into the sauce and the sauce to flow into the spaghetti: It's osmosis, and it's the way spaghetti Bolognese is supposed to taste.

SERVES

10

LEVEL *of* **DIFFICULTY**

WORTH THE EFFORT

REASONABLE

EASY

BOLOGNESE SAUCE
2 tbsp olive oil
4 lb/1.8 kg pork shoulder, ground
Coarse salt
4 oz/115 g prosciutto, ground or cut into small dice
6 carrots, cut into small dice
1 small red onion, cut into small dice
6 stalks celery, cut into small dice
3 garlic cloves, minced
2 tsp black peppercorns
1 tsp fennel seeds
1 tsp red pepper flakes
1 small bunch fresh thyme
1 bay leaf
½ cup/170 g tomato paste
1 cup/240 ml dry white wine
2 cups/480 ml low-sodium chicken stock, plus more if needed
One 28-oz/794-g can whole San Marzano tomatoes, crushed by hand, with juices reserved
Parmigiano-Reggiano rind (removed before grating)

1 tsp sugar
1 cup/240 ml heavy cream
2 tbsp red wine vinegar

2½ lb/1.2 kg spaghetti or rigatoni
2 cups/230 g freshly grated Parmigiano-Reggiano, plus more for serving
6 tbsp/90 ml olive oil
6 tbsp/85 g unsalted butter
½ cup/20 g chopped fresh flat-leaf parsley →

1. TO MAKE THE BOLOGNESE SAUCE: In a large Dutch oven or other heavy-bottomed pot, heat the olive oil over high heat and lightly brown the pork in batches, seasoning with salt each time. Don't overcrowd the pot, which will result in pale, steamed pork. But don't brown it too aggressively, either, as this will dry out the meat. It should simply lose its color and be evenly crumbled. Depending on the size of your pot, it will require roughly three batches. When each batch is finished, use a slotted spoon to transfer to a large plate or rimmed baking sheet. Do not discard the fat!

2. Turn the heat to medium and add the prosciutto, carrots, onion, celery, and garlic to the same pot and stir to coat in the rendered fat. Coarsely grind the peppercorns and fennel seeds with a mortar and pestle or crush with the flat side of a chef's knife blade. After the prosciutto and vegetables have cooked for a few minutes, stir in the ground pepper and fennel, the red pepper flakes, thyme, and bay leaf and cook for 1 minute to extract all the flavor from the herbs and spices.

3. Add the tomato paste and cook for a few minutes until it deepens in color, stirring often to prevent it from sticking to the bottom of the pot. Stir in the wine, scraping up any browned tomato paste or other bits from the bottom of the pot (a process called deglazing), and cook until the liquid is reduced by half.

4. Add the chicken stock and tomatoes with all their juices. Bring to a simmer and add the meat—including all the fat and juices that accumulated on the plate—and the Parmigiano rind. Add the sugar. Taste the sauce and add more salt, if needed. You don't need to simmer for hours; 45 minutes is plenty. It should look like chili. If the liquid ever evaporates to the point where the meat is not covered, add more stock sparingly.

5. After 40 minutes, skim off some but not all of the fat, add the cream, stirring thoroughly to incorporate, and simmer for another 5 minutes.

6. Remove the pot from the heat, and if you can find them, pick out the bay leaf, thyme stems, and any gooey remainder of the cheese rind. Taste once more for seasoning and add the vinegar to brighten the flavors.

7. In a large pot of abundantly salted boiling water, cook the pasta until al dente only, stirring often. Don't trust the instructions on the box; taste a noodle yourself and make sure it still has a lot of bite and is even a bit crunchy in the center. Scoop out about 1 cup/240 ml of the pasta cooking water. Drain the pasta and transfer to the sauce, adding a little bit of the pasta water into the sauce as well. (You might not need it all. It should be soupy enough that the rigatoni sink into the sauce, so the Bolognese is simmering around the tubes.)

8. When the sauce begins to thicken, 1 to 2 minutes, add the cheese, the 6 tbsp/90 ml olive oil, butter, and parsley. Remove the pan from the heat and stir, watching the sauce become velvety and rich. If the sauce becomes too dense with the addition of the cheese, a small splash of pasta water will loosen it up again. Serve immediately, with more grated cheese on the side.

I don't like making sachets with cheesecloth for the herbs; you can pick out the stems later. You'll get more flavor by cooking them naked with the vegetables.

A LOT OF TOMATO SAUCE

Go to a good supermarket for **FOUR 28-OZ/794-G CANS OF WHOLE SAN MARZANO TOMATOES** (the premium plum variety). Empty into a big bowl with their juices and crush the tomatoes by hand or with a potato masher. Place a large, heavy-bottomed pot over medium heat. Add about ¼ **CUP/60 ML OLIVE OIL** and **4 CRUSHED GARLIC CLOVES** and cook until the garlic starts to sizzle, 3 or 4 minutes. (Don't burn it. That will ruin the whole sauce.) Add the tomatoes in four portions, waiting until each comes to a simmer before adding the next. (This speeds up the cooking time.) Lower the heat, add **A FEW TORN BASIL LEAVES**, and simmer until the foaming subsides and the sauce looks a little oily, probably about 45 minutes. Let cool and store until ready to use. Add sautéed sliced mushrooms and cooked crumbled Italian sausage for a heartier sauce. **MAKES ABOUT 8 CUPS/2 L; SERVES 16.**

MUSSELS IN WHITE WINE

In a giant pot over medium heat, melt **4 TBSP/55 G UNSALTED BUTTER**. Add **4 GARLIC CLOVES** and **1 CUP/280 G QUARTER-CUT ONIONS**. Toss in a **TWO-FINGER PINCH OF RED PEPPER FLAKES** and **4 SPRIGS FRESH THYME**. When the aromatics are softened, after about 3 minutes— nothing smells better—add **2 CUPS/480 ML DRY WHITE WINE**. Simmer for about 1 minute to take out the "rawness" of the wine. At this point, you can turn the burner off; just return to a simmer when you're ready to cook. Add **4 LB/1.8 KG CLEANED, DEBEARDED MUSSELS** (see above) to the pot and mess them around a bit using a long wooden spoon. Cover and cook just until the mussels open, shaking the pot occasionally to help the process along, about 5 minutes. Transfer the mussels to serving bowls, pour in broth, and add a chunk of **BAGUETTE** —rip the bread rather than cutting it, for better soaking power. **SERVES 6 TO 8.** *Optional:* Dice a **6-IN/15-CM PIECE OF CHORIZO** and throw it in the pot with the aromatics to bloom the spices. Substitute **TWO 12-OZ/375-ML BOTTLES OF FINE BELGIAN BEER** for the wine.

SEAR: AN EAT-LIKE-A-MAN TUTORIAL

↓

SLAPPING POULTRY, seafood, or meat on a screaming-hot cooking surface for a short time deepens color, creates texture, and adds flavor—three noble goals. It also leaves behind beautiful little browned bits that you can easily make into a quick, rich pan sauce.

THE SCIENCE: Dry-heat cooking at a high temperature browns the surface of proteins due to a complex reaction between amino acids and reducing carbohydrates (or simple sugars) called the Maillard reaction, named for the French chemist Louis-Camille Maillard, who first reported the effect in 1912. Although the reaction is often shorthanded as "caramelization," the latter is actually a nonenzymatic browning process that depends exclusively on the molecular breakdown of sugars; the Maillard reaction occurs only when both protein and carbs are present. Anyway . . .

BEFORE SEARING, clear the stove top of any other pots and pans so they don't get grease splattered. The skillet should be heavy and ovenproof. It must be sized to fit what you're cooking: too small and the pan gets overcrowded, lowering the temperature and creating a braising rather than browning effect; too large and oil runs off to the sides and burns. The skillet must also be hot enough to sear the protein on contact, not only for a good finished appearance but to prevent any surface moisture from turning into steam and "sweating" the protein, ruining the chances of getting a crispy exterior.

BEFORE THE protein goes in, film the hot skillet with enough high-smoke-point oil—typically a neutrally flavored oil such as canola or grapeseed—to lightly coat the surface (typically no more than 2 tbsp in a 12-in/30.5-cm skillet). At the right temperature for searing, the oil will glisten and gently ripple across the surface without breaking down its molecular structure and burning.

THE MORE processed the oil, the higher its smoking point and the more neutral its flavor. Look at a bottle of expensive olive oil: Those floating "clouds" are the solids that remain behind after minimal processing. While bestowing the oil with distinctive flavor, those solids burn at higher heats. Pricy olive oil is best reserved for table use when you want to enjoy its full flavor, like a drizzle over roasted vegetables. Now look at a bottle of inexpensive refined oil like canola: Not much flavor but so clear, it's practically not there. You don't want to eat a piece of bread soaked in canola oil but it's good for high heat cooking.

CARVE FOWL

↓

DO NOT saw the breast the way they do in movies. Detach each breast along the backbone and at both ends, then remove it whole, like a tenderloin.

CRACK WINGS and drumsticks away from the body with your hands—this will expose the joints, which you can cut through easily (unlike bones).

DARK MEAT (the only real pleasure when it comes to turkey) is more of a hunting and gathering ritual. Cut, pull, dig. Be sure to turn the bird over in that search.

BE IT meat, seafood, or poultry, before searing, blot the meat dry on all surfaces with a paper towel and generously season with salt and pepper. Do this just before searing so the salt doesn't have time to draw the natural moisture to the surface, where it will steam, preventing a crisp exterior crust from forming.

7

BEFORE SEASONING, the skin on poultry and fish should be lightly brushed with oil—lightly!—to prevent sticking on contact (always sear skin-side down) and tearing (which reduces the beauty of the finished dish). The burner heat for poultry and fish is lower than the temperature used for meat: more on the medium-hot side. Because the fat under poultry skin releases moisture as it renders, shake the pan occasionally to displace the trapped liquid to prevent steaming and redistribute the cooking oil.

SANDWICH IDEAS FOR

LEFTOVER ROASTED CHICKEN

1 With Granny Smith apple slices and Saga blue cheese on pumpernickel

2 With Boursin cheese on toasted challah

3 With onion marmalade and shaved Cheddar on wheat toast

4 With bacon, avocado, and lettuce on seven-grain toast

SEARED SPATCHCOCKED CHICKEN

Spatchcocking a chicken by removing the backbone and flattening the bird (referred to in French as *crapoudine* for "in the style of a toad") allows the bird to cook evenly (meaning the breasts don't dry out before the thighs are done) and faster, resulting in crackly seared skin with the juiciness of a whole roasted bird. The flattened bird is infinitely easier to carve, and makes a great seasonal platter presentation, whether grilled and surrounded by sliced tomatoes in July, or seared and oven-roasted and served with mashed potatoes in January.

Any butcher will spatchcock a chicken for you, or you can learn to do it yourself: Remove the giblets and neck from inside the bird, and rinse and thoroughly blot dry inside and out. Place breast-side down on a cutting board and, using kitchen shears, cut along each side of the backbone lengthwise, from tail to neck. Pull the chicken open while applying pressure to each side, pushing down to flatten the breastbone. Trim excess fat from the edges, particularly the bottom of the bird. Using a sharp paring knife, cut horizontal slits along each side of the thigh bone, releasing it from the skin so the bird lies flat: better for searing and better for cooking. (At this point, the thigh bones act like a collar stay.)

Season **A SPATCHCOCKED CHICKEN (ABOUT 3 LB/1.4 KG BEFORE REMOVING BACK-BONE)** with **COARSE SALT** and **FRESHLY GROUND PEPPER**. Flip the bird over so it rests skin-side up on the cutting board. Fold the wingtips back and tuck the tips under so they don't prevent the breast skin from touching the bottom of the pan, which will prevent it from getting crispy. Preheat the oven to 375°F/190°C. Place the chicken skin-side down in a prepared 12-in/30.5-cm cast-iron or other heavy ovenproof skillet. Sear until the edges start to brown, 1 to 2 minutes, and then shake the pan to release any trapped moisture and redistribute the oil under the skin. Continue to sear until the skin is crispy and browned, 3 to 5 minutes. Transfer to the oven and roast until an instant-read thermometer inserted into the thickest part, without touching the pan, registers 165°F/70°C and the juices begin to run clear, about 35 minutes. Transfer the skillet to the stove top and flip the bird in the pan breast-side up. Let rest for 15 minutes, then carve and serve. **SERVES 2.**

SEARED STEAK

Preheat the oven to 350°F/180°C. Place **TWO 14- TO 16-OZ/400- TO 455-G SEASONED STRIP STEAKS** in a prepared ovenproof skillet and sear on the first side until crispy, about 3 minutes. Flip to sear the second side, which will take less time, about 2 minutes. Immediately transfer the skillet to the oven and cook until an instant-read thermometer inserted into the thickest part of the steak, without touching the pan, reads 130°F/54°C for medium-rare, about 6 minutes. Transfer the steaks to a carving board and let rest for about 5 minutes. (The temperature will continue to rise to about 135°F/60°C while the meat rests.) Carve into thin slices on the diagonal across the grain and serve immediately. SERVES 2.

SEARED SCALLOPS

Scallops are shucked on the boat. Some go into a cold-water storage container (often laced with a preservative like phosphorus) and although they last longer for the fishmonger, the absorbed liquid makes them heavier (you pay for that water weight) and reduces the intensity of flavor. These are sold as "wet scallops." Those that go into storage without water or preservatives are sold as "dry scallops." They don't last as long, which means they are generally the fresher option and the scallops retain their concentrated flavor.

Season **16 SEA SCALLOPS** with **SALT** and **PEPPER** and place half in a prepared skillet; it's especially essential not to overcrowd here, as the scallops will quickly steam and toughen). Sear on one side until beautifully browned, about 3 minutes. Add **A KNOB OF UNSALTED BUTTER** and **A SPRIG OR TWO OF FRESH THYME** (if you have it) and, when the butter is foamy, turn the scallops to brown the other side, about 1 minute. Immediately remove the scallops from the pan. Repeat with the second batch. Squeeze in the **JUICE OF ½ LEMON** and stir, scraping with your spoon to dissolve the tasty bits on the bottom of the pan. Pour the pan sauce over the scallops and serve. SERVES 8 AS AN APPETIZER.

Crunchy Shrimp Stir-Fry

I'm a big fan of fried garnishes—especially shallots—for extra texture, and I trace that love back to canned French's French Fried Onions. Like mothers all over the country, mine made the old-school green bean casserole, and I would eat half the can of fried onions before they could make it to the top of the casserole. Once you make the investment to try them, assembling the wok mix (an aromatic combination I call Thai *mirepoix* after the classic French mixture of carrots, celery, and onions that starts every stock) and stir-fry mix, you'll find out just how totally versatile and seasonally adjustable this recipe is. Go high end with lobster; scale it down with clams or mussels; add pea shoots in the summer, shaved squash in the fall, even thinly sliced cauliflower in the winter—there's no right or wrong. Only one rule reigns: Even if you don't have a wok, this is wok-style cooking. The aromatics should be finely and evenly cut for quick, uniform cooking, and you must keep them moving. This is not about slowing down to caramelize surface sugars. Add your ingredients bam-bam-bam and keep them dancing in the pan.

SERVES

2

(repeat to feed more)

LEVEL *of* **DIFFICULTY**

WORTH THE EFFORT

REASONABLE

EASY

✳

Rock shrimp are the smaller, deep-water, wild-caught crustacean cousin of pink, brown, and white shrimp, and have a milder, sweeter taste.

STIR-FRY SAUCE
2 tbsp oyster sauce
2 tbsp soy sauce
2 tbsp rice vinegar
1 tbsp fish sauce
1 tsp chile garlic sauce

4 oz/115 g rice noodles
2 tbsp canola oil

WOK MIX
2 tbsp peeled and minced fresh ginger
2 tbsp minced garlic
2 tbsp peeled and minced lemongrass
2 tbsp minced shallots

8 oz/230 g rock shrimp*
4 stalks asparagus, tough woody ends trimmed or snapped off, thinly sliced on the diagonal
2 scallions, thinly sliced
French's French Fried Onions for garnish

1. Mix up the Stir-Fry Sauce and set aside. Soak the noodles in a bowl of warm water according to the package directions, drain, and set aside, too.

2. Heat the oil in a heavy-bottomed skillet or wok over high heat. Add the Wok Mix and quickly toss and stir until aromatic and just tender, about 1 minute. Toss in the shrimp and cook, continuing to stir or shake the pan, until they pick up a hint of color, about 1 minute. Stir in the asparagus and scallions and quickly incorporate the soaked noodles, tossing and turning them to make sure all surfaces are coated.

3. Add the Stir-Fry Sauce and cook, tossing and stirring, just until the sauce has coated the noodles and no excess liquid is pooling in the pan, about 45 seconds.

4. Divide the stir-fry between two bowls, garnish with the fried onions, and serve immediately.

BILL TAIBE | THE WHELK | *Westport, Connecticut*

Boiled Lobster

Just about ten o'clock every morning, I get a lobster delivery from my local waterman, Norm Bloom, whose family has been pulling shellfish out of the Long Island Sound for three generations. When there's no stopover between their natural habitat and my kitchen, they retain their potent salinity, which plays against their natural sweetness. It's like nothing else in the world. When I boil lobster, I keep the focus on the fish. You make what's called a court bouillon—just seasoned cooking water—creating a saltwater base brightened by the acidity of wine and lemon, then enhanced with softer spices. But what really makes the difference is fresh bay leaves, because their piney astringency and citrusy essential oil are natural matches for shellfish. It's a simple thing with a big payoff.

If you aren't lucky enough to have Norm, find yourself a good fishmonger and make sure he holds up the lobsters so you can get a good look. Whether stored in a tank or on ice, the lobsters should not be lethargic; they should be alive and kicking. Before you spend good money on them, those lobsters better be snapping fresh.

SERVES

10

LEVEL *of* DIFFICULTY

WORTH THE EFFORT

REASONABLE

EASY

3 gl/11 L water
One 750-ml bottle dry white wine
3 lemons, halved
6 fresh bay leaves
2 tbsp coriander seed
2 tbsp white peppercorns
Handful of parsley stems (optional)
1 to 1¼ cups/170 to 255 g kosher salt
10 lobsters, 1¼ to 1½ lb/570 to
680 g each, claw bands on
Melted butter for serving

1. In a very large (5-gl/19-L) pot, combine all ingredients except the salt, lobsters, and butter and bring to a rolling boil over high heat. The water should fill the pot at least halfway. Add more if necessary. (The pot should be so deep that by the time the water comes to a boil, the aromatics and spices will be infused into the liquid.) →

When you get the lobsters home, placing them in the refrigerator under damp kitchen towels or newspapers will keep them moist and calm.

2. Add 1 cup/170 g of the salt to the heating water, stir to dissolve, then taste. It should taste very salty, like seawater. If it doesn't, add more salt, ¼ cup/40 g at a time. Cover the pot (it will come to a boil faster). Give yourself plenty of time for the water to heat up. It's okay to keep the water hot, ready, and waiting . . . the longer it hangs out, the more flavorful the "lobster bath" becomes.

3. Cook the lobsters in batches, five or six at a time. Using the lid as a shield (to avoid getting splashed with hot water), slide the lobsters, claw bands still on, into the water headfirst, like a plane taking a nosedive. (You may need to use tongs to help keep them submerged for the first minute or so.)

4. Although the aromatics may concentrate more in the meat after a 15-minute boil, lobster already tastes great, so I go for texture, pulling my lobsters at 8 minutes; that way you get really nice flavor and consistent tenderness. Using tongs, carefully remove the lobsters from the cooking liquid. (If you lift them sideways instead of pulling them straight up, the trapped water will drain easily.) Transfer to a platter or cutting board and cover tightly with aluminum foil to keep the lobsters hot while cooking the second batch. Let the water return to a full boil, then add the remaining lobsters and cook the same way.

5. Put the lobsters on large individual plates and serve hot, with picks, lobster crackers, bibs, piles of napkins, and lots of melted butter.

TIP

If you're uncertain of your timer, here's another way to tell if lobster is done: Remove the claw bands, pull back on the thumb claw, and wiggle it loose. If the cartilage pulls out easily and cleanly, your lobster is cooked.

SANDWICH IDEAS FOR
LEFTOVER LOBSTER

1 With mayo mixed with fresh tarragon on white sandwich toast

2 With bacon, tomato, and avocado on white sandwich toast

3 With curried mayo and watercress on a croissant

4 With coleslaw and salt-and-vinegar chips on a potato roll

CRACK A LOBSTER

↓

To minimize the work and mess of cracking and picking, you can do some of the breakdown work ahead of time for your guests, and arrange the prime parts on serving platters. (Use the same techniques to make lobster sandwiches, salads, or soups.)

STEP 1

Remove the claws: Place one hand on the body of the lobster to stabilize it and twist off each claw.

STEP 2

The goal is to remove the claw meat whole. Holding the claw at a 45-degree angle to the cutting board, strike the center of the shell with a chef's knife just until the blade is set like an ax in a tree. Twist the knife and break the shell open. (Don't use your best knife.)

STEP 3

Remove the tail: Cup the end of the tail with your palm (it tends to curl) and apply pressure with your thumb to the meatless part, then twist the tail from the body.

STEP 4

Cut down the back of the tail shell, keeping both hands on top of the knife blade. Pry open the shell and ease the tail meat out whole. Then remove the central vein along the back as you do with a shrimp.

TOM COLICCHIO | CRAFT | *New York, New York*

Salt-Baked Whole Fish with Buttermilk Chutney

The life of a chef requires its sacrifices—the hours are strange, the business unpredictable—and hobbies are the first things to go. But on rare mornings when I manage to steal a few hours, you'll find me offshore on my 26-foot Regulator, catching my dinner. I head out at sunrise and am back with my wife and boys by late morning, bearing bluefish or albacore, bonito or fluke. Sometimes I'll anchor over a wreck and fish for my favorite, black sea bass.

When I cook at home, my methods are always simple. One of my favorite ways to prepare sea bass is to encase it in salt and roast it. (If you're not in a position to catch your own, sea bass should be available at your grocery store or fish market. Otherwise, branzino or trout, even snapper, work well.) Salt-roasting is an ancient technique, probably because it has so much going for it: the salt crust seals water in to steam the fish in its own juices, seeps through the skin to season the flesh, and, as a bonus, allows for a big reveal in front of your guests when you break through the crust to expose a steaming, whole fish. And a big reveal never hurts.

SERVES

LEVEL *of* **DIFFICULTY**

WORTH THE EFFORT

REASONABLE

EASY

One 3-lb/1.4-kg whole sea bass
Some combination of fresh tarragon, thyme, parsley, chives, and/or rosemary leaves
10 egg whites
5 cups/850 g kosher salt*

BUTTERMILK CHUTNEY
1 leek, white and light green parts, halved and well rinsed
5 scallions, white and light green parts only
1 jalapeño chile, seeded
Olive oil
Small pinch of pink peppercorns
Small pinch of black onion seeds

Small pinch of mustard seeds
Small pinch of coriander seeds
Small pinch of fennel seeds
Big pinch of Vadouvan curry mix
¼ cup/60 ml buttermilk, or more if needed
½ lime
Coarse salt

*
I'm all for improvisation, but table salt does not work here.

1. Preheat the oven to 400°F/200°C.

2. Clip the fins off the sea bass and stuff its cavity with the herbs. In a large bowl, using your hands, mix together 2 of the egg whites for every 1 cup/ 170 g kosher salt until the concoction looks and feels like wet sand.

3. Spread a thin layer of the salt mixture on the bottom of a roasting pan or baking sheet, covering an area just larger than the fish. Lay the fish on top and fully pack it in the salt mixture until you have a smooth mound about the shape of a loaf of Italian bread. The fish should be totally sealed.

4. Place the fish in the oven and roast until an instant-read thermometer poked through the crust into the fish registers 120° to 125°F/48° to 50°C, 25 to 30 minutes.

5. WHILE THE FISH ROASTS, MAKE THE BUTTERMILK CHUTNEY: Finely chop the leek and thinly slice the scallions and jalapeño. Drizzle olive oil into a pan just to coat the bottom and place over medium heat. Add the vegetables and cook until softened but not browned.

6. Add all the spices and let them warm in the pan for about 1 minute. Remove the pan from the heat, let the contents cool slightly, and then add enough buttermilk to give the chutney a consistency like relish. Squeeze the lime into the mixture for a little more acid, and season with coarse salt.

7. When the fish is ready, the crust will be sand-colored and hard to the touch. You can break it open tableside (ta-da!), but you should probably return to the kitchen to deal with extracting and filleting the fish. The hardest part is lifting the fish out of the crust intact. Use two spatulas, one under the head and one under the body, to transfer it to a cutting board. Scrape or brush off any loose salt, then make a diagonal incision near the gills and another incision down the fish's back. This will allow you to lift off the top fillet using a spatula or spatulas, and transfer it, as intact as you can, to a platter. This will expose the spine. Lift out the bones, pulling up on the tail. If you're lucky, they'll come out in one piece, but comb the bottom fillet with your knife—most of the time you'll need to pick out stragglers. Next, using a spatula, carefully lift out the bottom fillet and transfer to the platter. Cut the top and bottom fillets in half and divide them (skin-side down) among serving plates or place them all on a platter. Scoop a spoonful of chutney onto the plates or platter and serve immediately.

BRYAN CASWELL | REEF | *Houston, Texas*

Whole Fish

This is a shallow-poaching technique for fish—something we do in the restaurant by the hundreds every week. The fish stays moist and contributes a significant amount of flavor to the liquid (called *cuisson*). Then, with a little butter and even less work, you've got a truly showy sauce. And it all happens in one pan. Your fishmonger will prepare it for you as described.

SERVES

LEVEL of DIFFICULTY

WORTH THE EFFORT

REASONABLE

EASY

One 1½- to 2½-lb/680- to 910-g
    whole fish such as sea bream,
    snapper, or striped bass, gutted,
    cleaned, scaled, and fins clipped
    off with scissors (with the
    exception of the tail)
Olive oil
Kosher salt
Cayenne pepper
3 shallots, thinly sliced
3 garlic cloves, chopped
3 sprigs fresh thyme
Handful of sliced scallions, white
    and green parts kept separate
Glug of dry white wine
½ to ⅔ cup/120 to 160 ml water
½ to ⅔ cup/120 to 160 ml clam juice
1 lemon, sliced
1 tbsp cold unsalted butter

1. Preheat the oven to 375°F/190°C. Choose a heavy-bottomed, ovenproof pan in which the fish will fit comfortably but snugly: a large cast-iron skillet, an oval-shaped Dutch oven, or a heavy-duty roasting pan with a flat bottom. You want the entire surface of the fish to come in contact with the pan.

2. Lay out the fish in the pan so that the head is to the right and the belly is facing you. With a sharp knife, make two slits about 1 in/2.5 cm below the gill plate, angling the blade away from the head at about 25 degrees and cutting straight to the bone (but not through it). Flip the fish over (head to the left and belly closest to you) and repeat the process. This will help shorten the cooking time in the thickest part of the fish.

3. Rub the entire fish liberally with olive oil. (You don't want the delicate skin to stick to the pan.) Liberally season the exterior as well as the interior belly and gill pouches with salt and cayenne. →

4. Get your pan ripping hot and liberally coat the bottom with a shallow puddle of olive oil. (Again, so the delicate skin doesn't stick. Fish looks better with its skin intact.) When the oil is rippling across the surface, gently place the fish in the pan and sear the first side until crisp. (Much depends on the heat and the pan, so timing can vary. Gently lift the fish to check.) Gently flip the fish and let the second side sear for about half the time it took for the first side. (This takes practice.)

5. Add the shallots, garlic, thyme, and white parts of the scallions to the pan. Let the aromatics sweat around the fish for a few minutes to release liquids. Add the wine and stir, scraping up any browned bits from the bottom of the pan. Give it a few seconds to fizzle down. Add equal parts of the water and clam juice, using just enough to come about one-third the way up the sides of the fish. Arrange a few lemon slices over the fish. Bring the liquid to a boil, then transfer the pan to the hot oven. When the blade of a knife can pierce through the fish without resistance, it's done. (I like to use a thin metal cake tester because it doesn't flake the fish.) The average cooking time is 12 to 15 minutes, but again, this will vary depending upon the pan and the heat.

6. Using two spatulas, transfer the fish to a platter and cover with aluminum foil to keep warm. Return the pan (it's hot, so be careful) to the stove top over low heat. Add the green parts of the scallions and bring the liquid to a simmer. Whisk in the cold butter to finish the sauce and give it a sheen.

7. Working from the belly side, use a thin-bladed knife to gently separate the top half of the fish. When properly cooked, it will slip right off the bone. Using a large spatula, carefully transfer the top fillet to a serving plate, using your hand like a spatula if necessary, and gently turning the fillet so that it is skin-side down.

8. Pick up the bone at the tail end and lift it toward the head as though you were pulling off a bandage, pressing down with the side of the knife blade to release the connective tissue below the gill plate if necessary. The entire bone frame will lift right off, looking like one of those fish skeletons in the Tweety Bird cartoons. Now lift out the bottom half, and carve both fillets into the number of portions you need. Spoon the sauce over each portion and serve immediately.

Most whole-fish recipes call for dry-roasting, stuffed with herbs and baking. But it usually turns out exactly that: dry. Caswell poaches fish in its liquidy natural habitat.

Chicken Cordon Bleu

This is the first—and most "gourmet"—recipe my mother taught me. Back in the era of hatha yoga and macramé owls, long before the current First Lady of New York state branded the idea of semi-homemade food, the Allen household lined up enthusiastically behind the use of Campbell's cream of mushroom soup as a sauce. Mom's cooking was, and is, delicious, but ours was not a household of croquembouche or food served in hollowed-out pumpkins. Think pork chops thrown in the Crock-Pot while we were at school, served with a side of Cronkite.

Is it tasty, this American approximation of the noble Chicken Cordon Bleu? Absolutely, to the extent I can remember the nuances of anything I cooked or did in the '70s. The texture is gloppy, the sodium content appalling, and the grayish hue isn't going to win points for presentation. But look, it's chicken breast stuffed with ham and gooey cheese, forever moist under its thick blanket of chickeny paste. You can prep it a day ahead and throw it in the oven while your guests nibble Swedish meatballs and spinach dip. Easy-peasy, George and Weezy. (Do people still say that?)

SERVES

LEVEL of DIFFICULTY

WORTH THE EFFORT

REASONABLE

EASY

12 boneless, skinless chicken breast halves
12 slices smoked ham
12 slices Swiss cheese (or, if you want to get fancy, Gruyère)
3 tbsp olive oil
Three 10¾-oz/305-g cans cream of mushroom soup

1. Preheat the oven to 350°F/180°C. Butter a 9-by-13-in/23-by-33-cm baking dish.

2. Place a chicken breast half between two sheets of wax paper and, using the flat side of a meat pounder, pound the chicken thin and flat. In the center of the flattened breast half, place a piece of ham, then a slice of cheese. Fold the left and right sides of the chicken over the filling, then roll it away from you to make a snug packet, keeping everything tucked in so the ham and cheese are fully enclosed (as if rolling a burrito). Seal with toothpicks. Repeat to fill and roll the rest of the chicken.

3. Heat the olive oil in a sauté pan over medium heat. Working in batches as needed to avoid crowding the pan, brown the chicken rolls on all sides, 2 or 3 minutes per side. Transfer the rolls to the prepared baking dish, pour the soup over, cover with aluminum foil, place in the oven, and bake until an instant-read thermometer inserted into the middle of a chicken roll reads 165°F/74°C, about 45 minutes. Check the temperature at 35 minutes or so. Remove from the oven and let rest for 5 minutes before serving, during which time the temperature will increase to 170°F/75°C.

Roast Chicken

We can all agree on a good roast chicken. What chefs can't always agree on is how to get there: brining, basting, roasting breast-side up, or breast-side down. I simply pour on some flavor and let the oven do the rest. What you get is a bird with crisp, almost shellacked skin (like Peking duck), in shades of teak to mahogany. The darker spots aren't burnt—that's the result of the caramelized sugars in the soy and honey. Which means that you and your oven did something right.

SERVES

LEVEL *of* DIFFICULTY

¼ cup/55 g unsalted butter, melted
¼ cup/60 ml soy sauce
¼ cup/85 g honey
One 3½-lb/1.6-kg good-quality chicken
Coarse salt and freshly ground black pepper
A few fresh herb sprigs such as thyme and rosemary (optional)

1. Preheat the oven to 325°F/165°C.

2. Combine the melted butter, soy sauce, and honey in a small bowl, stirring until well mixed.

3. Rinse the chicken inside and out with cold water, drain the excess liquid from the cavity, and pat dry inside and out with paper towels. The chicken should be bone dry. Any excess moisture creates steam in the oven and prevents the skin from crisping.

4. Rub the butter mixture all over the chicken, making sure to get it into the crevices around the legs and wings. Let the excess drip off. Sprinkle with salt and pepper. Stuff the fresh herbs (if using) into the cavity of the bird.

5. Place the chicken on a rack (if you have one) in a shallow roasting pan. There shouldn't be any excess liquid pooling on the bottom of the pan.

6. Place the chicken in the oven for 45 minutes. Turn on the stove vent and crank the heat to 425°F/220°C. Roast for another 10 minutes. (The sear comes at the end of the cooking process because at that point the fat has been rendered out and the skin is tighter, so you get a crispier end product.)

7. Remove the chicken and test for doneness. An instant-read meat thermometer inserted into the thickest part of a thigh (but without touching bone) should register about 160°F/70°C. Let the chicken rest for at least 10 minutes, then carve and serve immediately.

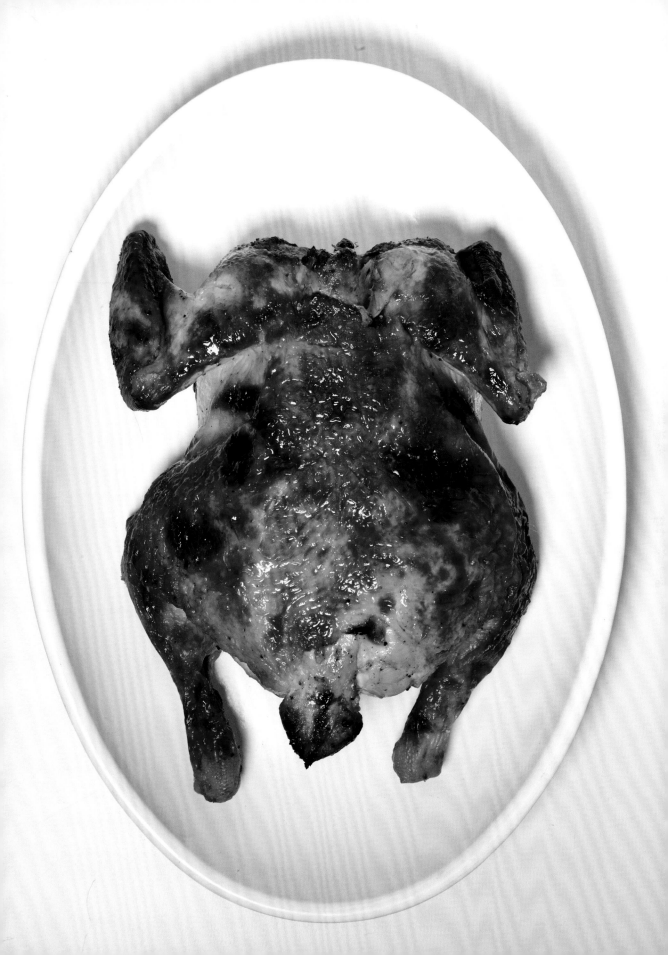

The Art of the One-Pot Meal

Stew is great. Takes all day, though.
A short-simmer one-pot meal follows a layered
framework—flavor on top of flavor on top of flavor—so that
everything blends together quickly and efficiently.

LAYER 1: ADD MEAT

The key is efficiency. Smaller cuts of poultry (darker, more flavorful thighs
and legs). Or try meat that comes with its own seasonings, like sausage taken out of
its casing so the seasonings ooze into the cooking liquid.

+

**LAYER 2:
CHOPPED AROMATICS**

Onions, shallots, leeks, and garlic, and firm vegetables like carrots or bell peppers, can hold up to
moving the meat around while you stir so they sink into the rendered fat. (Soft vegetables like zucchini
won't hold up well during the simmering period.) Because spices require direct heat to bloom their
flavor, sprinkle them over the vegetables, and nestle them into the fat with your spoon.

+

**LAYER 3:
LIQUID**

As the pot simmers, stock or canned tomatoes become your cooking medium and
should be a well-seasoned mix. This is the time to throw in sprigs of fresh thyme or rosemary
or oregano—the simmering liquid brings out the fragrant oils in the herbs.

+

LAYER 4: STARCH

This final layer is designed to soak up the cooking liquid, so it should be precooked, like canned beans, or quick-cooking, such as instant couscous or tiny pasta.

+

SETTLE THE POT:

When the cooking is done, remove the pot from the heat and let rest for 15 minutes or so to give the dish a chance to settle and intermingle its flavor elements. It's always a nice touch to hit your dish with a bit of final finesse by adding some sort of bright, fresh aromatic green such as snipped parsley or chives.

TIPS

One-pots may be an informal way to cook, but it still pays to write down what you use as you go. It's damn near impossible to re-create a great freestyle dish without a roadmap.

———

Get a pot with a larger cooking surface and short sides to maximize surface area. This way, more of your food touches the bottom of the pot and gets nice and brown while cooking, and everything simmers evenly because it's all spread out.

EXTREMELY EASY RECIPE

CHICKEN COUSCOUS ONE-POT

Trim the excess fat from **4 BONE-IN, SKIN-ON CHICKEN THIGHS.** Use your thumb to find the thigh bone and make slits on both sides with a paring knife so the thighs lie flat and get a better sear. Blot the thighs dry and season with **SALT** and **PEPPER.** In a preheated, lightly oiled, deep, heavy-bottomed skillet or Dutch oven, sear the thighs over high heat, skin-side down, until browned and crispy, shaking the pan occasionally to redistribute the fat. Turn the heat to medium and add **1 CHOPPED ONION, 4 OR 5 PEELED AND CHOPPED CARROTS,** and **½ CUP/90 G PITTED GREEN OLIVES** to the pan and distribute evenly. Sprinkle with **1 TSP EACH GROUND CUMIN AND GROUND CORIANDER,** shaking the pan so the spices sink into the fat and bloom flavor. Add **2 CUPS/ 480 ML CHICKEN STOCK, 2 SPRIGS FRESH THYME,** and **A PINCH OF RED PEPPER FLAKES.** Bring to a simmer and cook until the thighs are opaque through-out, 15 to 20 minutes. Add **½ CUP/60 G QUICK-COOKING COUSCOUS,** sprinkling it into the liquid and shaking the pan so it sinks in. Simmer until the couscous absorbs the liquid and is plumped and tender, about 5 minutes. Remove from the heat, sprinkle with **SNIPPED FRESH PARSLEY,** and let stand briefly to allow the flavors to mingle. Scoop into bowls and serve hot. **SERVES 4.**

Workhorse Chicken

Every party-recipe playlist should include a fail-safe chicken dish, that go-to recipe you've made so many times you know it by rote. These are your workhorse dishes, and they'll get the job done time and time again.

FRANCINE MAROUKIAN AND TONY AIAZZI

CHICKEN ROASTED OVER BACON STUFFING

This holiday-spirited dish delivers crowd-pleasing chicken and stuffing in an easy-to-serve casserole: no browning, no carving.

6 oz/170 g mildly smoked slab bacon, cut into 4 slices about ¼ in/6 mm thick

2 small red onions, diced

6 stalks celery, diced

Coarse salt and freshly ground black pepper

1 tbsp Bell's poultry seasoning

2½ cups/600 ml chicken stock

3 extra-large eggs, lightly beaten

1 loaf country-style bread, cut into 1-in/2.5-cm cubes and lightly toasted

½ cup/60 g coarsely chopped fresh flat-leaf parsley

One 3-lb/1.4-kg chicken, cut into eight serving pieces (2 wings, 2 legs, 2 thighs, and 2 breast halves), rinsed under cool water and patted dry with paper towels

Vegetable oil for brushing

1. In a 12-in/30.5-cm skillet over medium heat, cook the bacon until golden brown and crispy, 4 to 6 minutes. Stir the onions and celery into the bacon along with 1 tsp salt, pepper to taste, and the poultry seasoning and sauté until the vegetables are just starting to soften, about 5 minutes.

2. Pour in the chicken stock and bring to a simmer, then immediately remove from the heat so the stock doesn't reduce. Let stand for 5 minutes to allow the flavors to infuse. Transfer the contents of the skillet to a large bowl and let cool so the eggs can be added without cooking them. When the seasoning mixture has cooled, add the eggs and stir to incorporate. Add the bread cubes and parsley and fold to combine. Let stand for 15 to 20 minutes so the bread can fully absorb the liquid.

3. Preheat the oven to 375°F/190°C.

4. Transfer the dressing to an 8-by-13-in/20-by-33-cm baking pan and pack it into the pan loosely. Season the chicken pieces on both sides with salt and pepper, and press each piece into the dressing, skin-side up. Brush the skin lightly with oil. Place in the oven and roast until the skin is crispy brown and the internal temperature registers 140°F/60°C on an instant-read thermometer, 45 to 50 minutes. Let the chicken rest for 10 minutes, then serve.

SERVES 6

COFFEE-RUBBED CHICKEN-THIGH SANDWICHES

Behold the glory when we turn our attention from breasts to thighs.

SPICE RUB*
1 tsp coarse salt
1 tsp chili powder
½ tsp freshly ground black pepper
½ tsp ground coffee
½ tsp ground cumin
**½ tsp dried orange peel
granules (jarred)**
Olive oil

4 bone-in, skin-on chicken thighs
**6 oz/170 g pepper Jack cheese,
thinly sliced**
4 English muffins, split
½ ripe avocado, thinly sliced
**1 red, ripe tomato, cut into slices
¼ in/6 mm thick**

1. Preheat the oven to 325°F/165°C. Line a baking sheet with aluminum foil or parchment paper.
2. **TO MAKE THE SPICE RUB:** In a large bowl, combine the salt, chili powder, pepper, ground coffee, cumin, and orange peel. Stir in just enough olive oil to make a paste.
3. Add the chicken thighs to the bowl with the spice rub and toss to coat evenly. Arrange the chicken on the prepared baking sheet, skin-side up. Roast for 45 minutes, giving the fat enough time to render out and crisp the skin. (The meat will also be fork-tender by then.) Remove the chicken from the oven and set aside to cool. (If you are going to use the chicken immediately to make sandwiches, leave the oven on.)
4. When the chicken has cooled enough to handle, turn the thighs skin-side down and place in an ovenproof skillet. Using a paring knife, make slits along each side of the thigh bones, then carefully pull out the bones, leaving the meat intact. (At this point, you can store the chicken in an airtight container in the refrigerator for up to 2 days.)
5. Turn the thighs skin-side up and top with the cheese. Place back in the hot oven just long enough to melt the cheese, about 10 minutes. While the cheese is melting, toast the English muffins.
6. Shingle the slices of avocado on the bottom halves of the English muffins, top each with a coffee-roasted chicken thigh, and finish with a slice of tomato. Close with the top halves of the English muffins. Press down lightly to seal. Cut in half and serve immediately.

SERVES 4
(multiply to feed masses)

You may substitute ¼ cup/35 g store-bought coffee spice rub. Use a complex aromatic spice mix such as a Moroccan combination to bring out the best in chicken's darker meat, mixed with enough olive oil to make a paste.

MITCHELL ROSENTHAL | **SALT** | *San Francisco, California*

Grilled Pork Chops with Pickled Cherry Peppers, Rosemary, and Garlic

Lean, boneless cuts of meat have a tendency to dry out, and that's why brining—immersing the chops in what amounts to a seasoned saltwater bath—is your friend. As opposed to seasoning the surface of the meat, brining not only allows the seasoning to penetrate the whole chop, it aids in retaining moisture. Ideally you want the pork to sit in the brine for at least twenty-four hours, but if you plan on pork chops for dinner and only have time to toss them in the brine before you go to work, they'll still be better off.

SERVES

LEVEL of DIFFICULTY

WORTH THE EFFORT

REASONABLE

EASY

BRINE
10 cups/2.3 L water
2 tbsp fennel seeds, crushed
4 bay leaves, crumbled
2 tbsp peppercorns
4 sprigs rosemary
6 garlic cloves, coarsely chopped
¾ cup/170 g sugar
½ cup/100 g coarse salt

Ten 10- to 12-oz/280- to 340-g boneless center-cut pork chops, about 1¼ to 1½ in/3 to 4 cm thick

PICKLED CHERRY PEPPERS*
12 cherry peppers
Pinch of coarse salt
1½ tsp olive oil
1½ cups/360 ml white vinegar

¾ cup/150 g sugar
Leaves from 2 sprigs fresh rosemary

¼ cup/60 ml canola oil
4 large garlic cloves, slivered
4 sprigs rosemary
½ cup/115 g unsalted butter

While you can use jarred cherry or Peppadew peppers (or, if you want extra heat, Calabrian chiles) for this recipe, pickling your own adds a notch to your belt and gives you something to do while the pork is in the brine.

1. TO MAKE THE BRINE:
Place 1 cup/240 ml of the water in a saucepan and add the fennel seeds, bay leaves, peppercorns, rosemary, and garlic. Bring to a simmer, then remove from the heat. Let cool to room temperature, 10 to 15 minutes. Add the remaining 9 cups/2.1 L water, sugar, and salt and stir until dissolved and well combined.

2. Rinse the pork chops and pat dry with paper towels. Place in a clean bowl. Pour the brine over the chops and place a plate on top to keep the chops submerged. Refrigerate for 24 hours.

3. WHILE THE CHOPS ARE BRINING, MAKE THE PICKLED CHERRY PEPPERS:
Preheat the broiler. Cut the peppers in half and remove the seeds. Toss the peppers with the salt and olive oil. Spread the peppers on a baking sheet, skin-side up, and broil for about 5 minutes, until the skins begin to blister and the peppers soften slightly. Remove from the oven and set aside. Put the vinegar, sugar, and rosemary in a small saucepan, bring to a gentle boil over medium-high heat, and cook for 2 to 3 minutes. Pack the peppers into a jar and pour in the hot pickling liquid. Let cool to room temperature. The peppers are now ready to eat, or screw the lid on the jar tightly and store in the refrigerator for up to 4 weeks.

4. Prepare a medium-hot grill. (Place your palm about 4 in/10 cm above the grate. If you can stand it for 4 or 5 seconds before you have to pull away, that's a pretty good approximation of medium-hot.)

5. While the coals are getting hot, take the chops out of the brine, rinse them thoroughly under cold water, and pat them dry with paper towels. Discard the brine.

6. When the moment of medium-hot has arrived, place the chops on the grill. Give them a little elbow room. Let them cook for 6 or 7 minutes per side. (You want the internal temperature at about 145°F/60°C.) The sugars from the brining process will caramelize beautifully, giving you bold, slightly charred grill marks across the chops.

7. When they're done, transfer the chops to a platter and loosely cover with aluminum foil. Let them rest. It's important. This simple step lets the proteins relax and reabsorb moisture, distributing the meat's juices evenly throughout. It might be the best few minutes you've ever spent.

8. Meanwhile, heat the canola oil in a very large pan over medium heat. When the oil is shimmering, add the garlic and rosemary sprigs. Cook for 2 minutes or so, shaking the pan a little throughout. Add about 12 pickled pepper halves and the butter, again, keeping it moving. Stir until the butter is melted and the peppers, rosemary, and garlic are slightly browned.

9. Place the chops on plates and top each with the remaining pepper halves and then drizzle with plenty of the pan juices.

10. Eat.

Chile Verde

***Chile verde*, true** to its name, relies on green and poblano chiles spiked with jalapeños for flavor and heat. So please resist the urge to sling in chili powder, cumin, cinnamon, or any of those other "secret" ingredients you add to your regular red-chili recipe.

SERVES

LEVEL *of* DIFFICULTY

WORTH THE EFFORT

REASONABLE

EASY

6 tbsp/90 ml olive oil

4 large yellow onions, chopped

10 garlic cloves, minced

6 fresh jalapeño chiles, stemmed and minced, seeds removed if you like less heat

2 stalks celery, diced

4 lb/1.8 kg boneless pork shoulder, patted dry and cut into ½-in/ 12-mm cubes

5 tsp dried Mexican oregano

5 cups/1.2 L chicken stock

8 canned tomatillos, drained and puréed

2 small potatoes, peeled and grated

2 tsp coarse or kosher salt

4 canned roasted poblano chiles, cut into ½-in/12-mm strips

1½ cups/180 g canned green chiles (I like Hatch brand), drained

2 ripe avocados, pitted, peeled, and finely chopped

4 ripe plum tomatoes, seeded and finely chopped

1. In a large, heavy-bottomed pot over medium heat, heat the olive oil. Add the onions, garlic, jalapeños, and celery and cook, stirring occasionally, until the celery is softened, about 10 minutes.

2. Add the pork and oregano and cook, stirring often, until the pork loses its color, 8 to 10 minutes. Add the stock, tomatillos, potatoes, and salt and bring to a boil. Lower the heat and simmer, partially covered, for 90 minutes, stirring occasionally.

3. Add the poblanos and green chiles, return to a simmer, and cook, still partially covered and stirring often, until the pork is tender, another 30 to 45 minutes. Ladle into warm bowls, top with the avocado and tomato, and serve immediately.

SEAMUS MULLEN | TERTULIA | *New York, New York*

Cubano-Flavored Pork

You can get authentic-tasting Cubano pork—without roasting the entire pig—by brining the roast before cooking it. This technique helps tenderize the meat; and if you marinate the leftovers (see Tip), the meat will keep for up to 7 days in the refrigerator. That's a good thing—one pork roast can easily provide enough meat for a week's worth of sandwiches.

SERVES

LEVEL of DIFFICULTY

WORTH THE EFFORT

REASONABLE

EASY

BRINE
4 cups/960 ml water
½ cup/100 g kosher salt
½ cup/100 g sugar
1 tbsp coriander seeds
1 tbsp mustard seeds
3 bay leaves
3 dried chile peppers (preferably Guindilla, if you can find them, but poblano or any other hot variety will work)

4 lb/1.8 kg boneless Berkshire pork loin
Coarse salt and freshly ground black pepper
6 tbsp/90 ml olive oil

1. TO MAKE THE BRINE: Combine all the ingredients in an extra-large zippered plastic bag or brining bag.

2. Add the pork loin to the brine and refrigerate overnight.

3. Preheat the oven to 200°F/95°C.

4. Remove the loin from the brine, rinse, and pat dry with paper towels. Season with salt and pepper. Discard the brining liquid.

5. Place a sturdy flameproof roasting pan over two stove-top burners. Add the olive oil and heat until hot but not smoking. Add the roast and sear to brown on all sides.

6. Transfer the pan to the oven and roast for 3 hours, or until an instant-read thermometer inserted into the thickest part of the roast registers 150°F/65°C.

7. Remove from the oven and transfer to a carving board. Let rest for about 10 minutes. Carve across the grain on the diagonal into slices of the desired thickness to serve.

To store leftover roast, place in a container with a tight-fitting lid and cover the sliced pork in olive oil; fresh herbs such as thyme, rosemary, and sage; whole garlic cloves; and red pepper flakes. The meat will keep in this marinade in the refrigerator for about 7 days.

Roasted Pork Chops with Cipollini Onions, White Beans, and Escarole

The escarole and beans can be made in advance and reheated gently with a drizzle of fresh olive oil until warm.

SERVES

10

LEVEL *of* DIFFICULTY

WORTH THE EFFORT

REASONABLE

EASY

MARINADE

4 sprigs fresh rosemary

5 garlic cloves, crushed

½ cup/120 ml extra-virgin olive oil

10 shoulder or loin pork chops,
    1½ in/4 cm thick

Coarse salt and freshly ground black
    pepper

About ¼ cup/60 ml canola oil

1 tbsp unsalted butter

½ cup/120 ml olive oil

10 cipollini onions, peeled

3 tbsp sugar

¾ cup/180 ml red wine vinegar

2 sprigs fresh rosemary

2 cups/480 ml chicken stock

3 garlic cloves, minced

2 lb/910 g escarole, cored, washed, dried,
    and separated into leaves

3 cups/780 g cooked white beans

Juice of 1 lemon

1. TO MAKE THE MARINADE:
Combine the rosemary, garlic, and extra-virgin olive oil in a large zippered plastic bag.

2. Add the pork chops and turn to coat. Refrigerate for at least 8 hours, or up to 3 days, turning the bag occasionally. When you plan to cook the chops, remove them from the fridge and bring to room temperature.

3. Remove the chops from marinade, pat dry with paper towels, and season on both sides with salt and pepper. Heat a large cast-iron skillet over medium-high heat. Working in batches to avoid overcrowding the pan, add 1 or 2 tbsp of the canola oil for each batch and, once hot, add the pork chops. Cook for 3 minutes, then flip and cook for 3 minutes longer. Transfer the seared pork chops to a large baking sheet as each batch is finished. When all of the chops are seared, set the baking sheet aside at room temperature.

4. Preheat the oven to 325°F/165°C.

5. In a heavy-bottomed saucepan over medium heat, melt the butter with ¼ cup/60 ml of the olive oil. When hot, add the onions, season with salt and pepper, and brown all over, using tongs to turn as needed. Sprinkle with the sugar and stir in the vinegar, scraping up any browned bits from the bottom of the pan. Cook until the liquid is evaporated. Add the rosemary and chicken stock. Return to a simmer and cook for 20 minutes, or until the onions are tender. Remove from the heat. Using a slotted spoon, transfer the onions to a bowl and set aside. Reserve the liquid in the pan as a sauce for the pork chops.

6. Place the baking sheet holding the pork chops directly into the oven and bake for 10 to 12 minutes, turning once. The pork is cooked when an instant-read thermometer inserted into the thickest part of a chop registers 155°F/68°C. Remove from the oven, tent loosely with aluminum foil, and let rest.

7. Meanwhile, in a large skillet or sauté pan over medium heat, heat the remaining ¼ cup/60 ml olive oil. When the oil is hot, add the garlic and escarole and sauté for 1 minute, or until the escarole is wilted. Add the white beans and sauté until heated through, about 5 minutes longer. Season with salt and pepper and toss with the lemon juice.

8. Put a chop on each plate and top with the white bean–escarole mixture and onion. Drizzle with the onion jus and serve immediately.

SANDWICH IDEAS FOR

LEFTOVER ROAST PORK

1 With sunny-side-up eggs and roasted tomato salsa on a Kaiser roll

2 With dressed arugula, sliced fresh mozzarella, and sliced tomatoes on a sub roll

3 With sautéed greens and grated Parmesan on toasted crusty bread

4 With pickled hot peppers and shredded lettuce with Italian dressing on a hoagie roll

Braised Pork Shepherd's Pie

When it comes to cooking for a crowd, you want a recipe that gets right to the point. Shepherd's pie is a rustic British dish typically made with mutton or beef, but my modern version uses pork shoulder. Because the shoulder itself has plenty of flavor, you can braise it in water instead of stock. Also, I use Yukon gold potatoes because they have a medium-starch makeup and can better absorb butter and cream. When topping the casserole with the potatoes, here's a good technique: Add more mashed potatoes than you need, spreading them over the surface (without disturbing the mixture underneath and getting little pieces of vegetables caught in the potatoes), and then remove the excess.

SERVES

12

LEVEL of DIFFICULTY

WORTH THE EFFORT

REASONABLE

EASY

Ask the butcher for a roast with a good meat-to-fat ratio, as the fat will melt during the long cooking period and help to tenderize the pork.

One 4½-lb/2-kg pork
    shoulder roast*
Coarse salt
5 carrots, peeled and diced
4 stalks celery, diced
4 small yellow onions, diced
4 garlic cloves, smashed
8 black peppercorns
5 tbsp/85 g tomato paste
9 large Yukon gold potatoes
12 tbsp/170 g cold unsalted
    butter, cut into 12 pieces
3 to 4 cups/720 to 960 ml
    heavy cream
Freshly ground black pepper
1½ cups/285 g frozen peas,
    thawed

1. Preheat the oven to 325°F/165°C.

2. Season the meat with 1 tbsp plus 1 tsp salt.

3. In the bottom of a large Dutch oven or other ovenproof pot with a tight-fitting lid, combine the carrots, celery, onions, garlic, peppercorns, tomato paste, and 1 tbsp salt and stir to mix well. Place the pork on top. Add water to cover the pork about three-fourths of the way up the sides, cover the pot, and bring to a boil over medium-high heat, about 15 minutes. Immediately transfer the pot to the oven and braise the roast until tender and falling apart, 2 to 2½ hours.

4. When the pork is almost done, peel the potatoes and cut into large chunks (about 2 in/5 cm). Place in a large pot, cover with cold water, bring to a boil, and adjust heat to keep the water boiling without overflowing. Cook until the potatoes are fork-tender, about 10 minutes. →

Drain in the pot, then while the potatoes are still hot, add 2 tsp salt, the butter (piece by piece), and the cream (slowly), mashing the potatoes with an old-fashioned potato masher as you go. The texture should be as silky as possible. Taste, adjust the seasoning with salt and pepper, cover, and let rest in a warm spot near the oven. (The potatoes must be warm in order to be spreadable.)

5. Remove the pork from the oven and let rest in its liquid for 20 to 25 minutes to ensure it will not get dry. Transfer the pork to a cutting board. Using a slotted spoon, carefully transfer the vegetables to an extra-large bowl and add the peas. (Reserve the braising liquid in the pot.) When the roast is cool enough to handle, cut it into small bite-size cubes or just tear it into shreds using two forks. Add to the bowl with the vegetables and toss gently to combine, then add enough of the cooking liquid to moisten the meat mixture without letting it get "stewy" (¼ to ½ cup/60 to 120 ml). Taste and adjust the seasoning again.

6. Preheat the broiler.

7. You can use any number of baking dishes or ovenproof casseroles you might have handy, in a range of sizes or shapes, with this guideline: The pan must allow for filling that is about 2 in/5 cm deep plus a thick blanket of potatoes on top.

8. Transfer the meat mixture to the pan or pans and carefully spread the potatoes over the top, completely covering the meat. Slide under the broiler to lightly crisp the top. Watch carefully—this will take only about 60 seconds. Serve immediately.

To reheat, first bring the dish to room temperature, then place it in a preheated 325°F/165°C oven until heated throughout.

The Pig Roast

JOHN MARIANI

FOR THE PAST few years, on my birthday, I've held a pig roast in the backyard, an event that affords me the company of a dozen good friends for whom the uniqueness of the enterprise is at least as enticing as the eating of the pig, which Charles Lamb, in his essay "A Dissertation upon Roast Pig," called "animal manna." It is *not* an intimate affair. Everyone pitches in, making drinks, fetching utensils, and the all-important standing around the grill that males have been doing for millennia, muttering questions like "What kinda wood you using?" "Think you better give it another basting?" and "When's the damn thing gonna be done?"

The sight of even a baby pig—twenty pounds is good-sized—its head, tail, and trotters intact, eyes staring at you, lends the preliminaries of preparation a ritualistic cast. Then, as the pig browns and the smoke twirls and puffs from the spit, the aromas drive your appetite to a frenzy and you feel waves of emptiness in your gut. When the pig is done and everyone sits down to pluck morsels of creamy flesh, sweet fat-cuddled ribs, and crackling shards of mahogany-colored skin from the platter, dipping the meat in a sauce of puréed garlic, onion, and orange juice, some people swoon, others moan, and some sit in silence, just smiling and shaking their heads. There's no question that people will eat too much, and no doubt that there will be pig left over. I dissuade people from taking any home, for tomorrow I'll enjoy the meal all over again, just me and the pig and a glass of red wine. And I forget all about the fact that I've grown older by a year.

Roast Pork Arista

Tying your roast creates uniformity, not only in cooking time but in appearance as well, so the meat looks good on both the outside and the inside (with an even internal temperature) and carves well.

SERVES

8

LEVEL *of* **DIFFICULTY**

WORTH THE EFFORT

REASONABLE

EASY

Kosher salt

One 7-rib bone-in pork rib roast, * **frenched (the meat cut away from the end of each rib, exposing the bone), with the chine and feather bones removed (ask your butcher to do this)**

RUB

¼ cup/30 g ground fennel seeds
3 tbsp finely chopped fresh rosemary
2 tbsp minced garlic
2 tbsp freshly ground black pepper
1 tbsp red pepper flakes

1. Salt the roast abundantly all over, remembering to rub the granules between the bones and on the broad ends of the meat. You need enough to season the thickness of the meat, and some will fall off during the process.

2. TO MAKE THE RUB: In a small bowl, stir together all the rub ingredients.

3. Cover the roast with the rub, making sure all surfaces and crevices get their share of the spices. Tie up the roast, using a butcher's slipknot. Wrap the roast in plastic wrap and refrigerate overnight.

4. Preheat the oven to 425°F/220°C. Unwrap the roast and let it sit at room temperature while the oven is preheating.

5. Place the roast in a low-sided roasting pan to maximize the browning area and sear in the hot oven until a crust forms, about 20 minutes. Lower the oven temperature to 275°F/135°C, popping open the door for a few minutes to help dissipate the internal heat. Close the oven door and roast until an instant-read thermometer inserted into the thickest part of the meat registers 135°F/57°C, about 15 minutes per 1 lb/455 g.

6. Remove the roast from the oven and transfer to a carving board. Let rest for 30 minutes. Snip and remove the strings with a sharp knife. Letting the bones act as your portioning guide, carve into eight thick slices. Serve immediately.

Rather than ordering your roast by weight, plan on 1 rib per serving. This 7-bone roast feeds 8, assuming a couple of people don't need an entire bone.

Gyro-Style Meat Loaf

There are plenty of great recipes kicking around for Mom's meat loaf. This is not one of them. Instead, we take traditional Middle Eastern street food you usually find rotating on a vertical spit and fit it into a loaf pan. Adding bulgur wheat absorbs internal liquid and helps the meat loaf keep its rectangular shape so you can serve a nice thick slab with rice pilaf or slide thin slices into a warm pita, layering in more flavor with spicy yogurt and tart cucumber salad.

SERVES

8

LEVEL *of* **DIFFICULTY**

WORTH THE EFFORT

REASONABLE

EASY

MEAT LOAF
1½ lb/680 g ground lamb
1½ lb/680 g ground beef
1 yellow onion
1 tbsp coarse salt
½ tsp freshly ground black pepper
Heaping 2 tbsp za'atar*
2 tbsp dried parsley
1 tsp granulated garlic
3 large eggs, lightly beaten
⅓ cup/50 g quick-cooking bulgur wheat
Olive oil for drizzling

SALAD
1 cucumber, peeled and thinly sliced
1 small red onion, thinly sliced
3 tbsp extra-virgin olive oil
1 tbsp white wine vinegar
Pinch of dried parsley
Pinch of dried mint

HARISSA-YOGURT SAUCE
Harissa**
½ cup/120 ml whole-milk plain
    Greek yogurt

Za'atar is a
Middle Eastern
spice mix
that typically
contains dried
oregano, thyme,
marjoram,
sesame seeds,
and sumac.
It is available
at specialty
markets.

Harissa is
a Tunisian
hot sauce,
also sold at
specialty
markets.

1. TO MAKE THE MEAT LOAF:
Preheat the oven to 375°F/190°C.
Lightly coat a 9-by-5-in/23-by-
13-cm loaf pan with olive oil. (If you
have a loaf pan with a perforated
insert for draining fat, use it.)
2. Combine the ground lamb and
beef in a large bowl and set aside.
3. Rest a box grater in a medium
bowl. Using the large grating holes,
grate the onion, allowing all of the
onion pulp and juice to go into
the bowl (partly for the bulgur to
absorb). (Depending on the onion,
this can really clear the room, so
get it done as quickly and efficiently
as possible with no one around who
you wouldn't want to see you cry.)
4. Add the salt, pepper, za'atar, parsley, and granulated garlic to the bowl
with the onion and stir to mix well.
Add the onion mixture to the meat
mixture, along with the eggs and
the bulgur. Using your hands, mix
together gently until the mixture is
well combined.
5. Pack the meat mixture into
the prepared pan, pressing down
firmly—especially in the corners,
so there are no air pockets. Drizzle
olive oil over the top and spread
out to evenly coat. Bake until an

instant-read thermometer inserted
into the middle of the loaf registers
150°F/65°C, about 50 minutes. The
meat should be firm and springy
when pressed with a fingertip.
**6. WHILE THE MEAT LOAF
BAKES, MAKE THE SALAD:**
Combine the cucumber and red
onion in a small serving bowl. In a
separate small bowl, whisk together
the olive oil, vinegar, parsley, and
mint. Dress the vegetables with the
vinaigrette and toss to coat evenly.
**7. TO MAKE THE HARISSA-
YOGURT SAUCE:** In a serving
bowl, simply mix as much of
the harissa as you can handle
into the yogurt.
8. Slice the meat loaf, top each
slice with harissa-yogurt sauce, and
serve with the salad alongside.

Done

TOM JUNOD

**HEN YOU START** doing your own cooking, it's like when you start having sex—you can finally start figuring out what you *like*. There's a tendency to characterize cooking as a kind of thralldom (the phrase "slave to the kitchen" comes to mind), but really, all those hours prepping and chopping, all that time spent over the hot stove, are more about freedom than they are about responsibility. Indeed, a lot of food writing now is as overheated as sex writing was thirty years ago because of the mistaken notion that there's a lot at stake every time you light the fire, with an existential emphasis on performance. The hell with that. Sure, in theory, both sex and cooking are about nothing less than human survival, and so it's easy to burden them with big thoughts. But in practice, they're about human ease, and the time we take with each other, and the small pleasures of being alert to individual preference. On one level, it's easy to screw up; on another, it's nearly impossible, because even the worst meal satisfies hunger, and the best goes past the paltry satisfactions of technique and sophistication to remind us of our corporeal innocence.

No one would call me a great cook, but over years of cooking, for me, confidence has replaced ambition. Because I actually like cooking for people, people like what I cook for them. It's that simple—except for the one crucial question of competence that underlies all cooking and haunts every cook. It's the question that marks you as a grown-up in the kitchen once you can answer it, and ironically it's the same question you had about cooking when you were a child: When is it done?

There are only three questions that matter in the kitchen if you're cooking and not baking. The first is how good are your ingredients; the second is how much salt to add; and the third is how long to cook whatever it is you're cooking—the question of *doneness*. You can get by with guesswork with the first two, and you can find your answers with money or a tablespoon. The question of doneness, however, is a mystery, and so it resists approximation and precision in equal measure. Indeed, it's the only question about cooking that passes for an existential one, because it takes time into account and can be answered only with instinct or experience. After all, even if you have a thermometer, you can't see inside what you're cooking; at some level, you just have to *know*. If you do, you can get away with just about anything. If you don't—if you, like my mom, cook pot roast and salmon fillets for about the same amount of time—you become an anxious cook, which puts you halfway on the path to becoming an ungenerous one.

So how do you know when food is done? Cookbooks try to tell you. They say that chicken is done "when the juices run clear," the fish "when the flesh is opaque when you insert the point of a knife." But the decision is at once simpler and more complicated because, of course, the food is done before you even try cooking it, or, to be more exact, it is done *with*. If it's from a beast, the beast no longer breathes; if from a fish, the fish no longer swims; if from a plant, the plant no longer grows. Its first life is finished, and its second one is in your hands.

What you're cooking is never going to be anything but dead, but as long as you're cooking it, it's also coming to some kind of fruition—which is why the question of when it's done makes all the others seem insignificant. Doneness is nothing less than destiny, and so deciding it is not so much a matter of recognizing when juices run clear as it is a matter of recognizing the difference between tough and tender, between cheap and expensive, between summer and winter. In general, you cook long in the winter, short in the summer. You cook long on the cheap, short when you can afford it. And yet no amount of helpful hints can account for the difference between what a rural Southern cook and a Whole Foods habitué might do with a bunch of kale, or between what you and your *nonna* might consider a suitable tomato sauce. Food's not done until it *yields* something, maybe its soul or maybe just its secrets, and how long you're willing to wait for that to happen is a secret all your own.

But maybe I'm claiming ineffability for what is essentially a chemical reaction, as clear-cut as any other. Lately, science has deepened the art of cooking by making the basics of cooking—the response of fat and protein to heat—predictable, and by defining "doneness" in precise molecular terms. And you don't need to be a scientist to realize a few basics: brown is almost always good, and black is almost always bad; you shouldn't be any more timid with fish than you would be with steak; it's easier to eat an overcooked chicken than an undercooked one; and anyone who tells you that you can't overcook a pot roast or dry out a slow-cooked pork shoulder is lying. The food you're cooking has, in a sense, already been murdered once; cooking gets easy once you realize that your only responsibility is to not murder it again. A scientist might have a more exact way of saying that, but he wouldn't have a better word than the one we use for food that comes magically alive to taste and smell and texture and thus lets you know when the fire is finished with it and it is finished with the fire:
Done.

Slow-Roasted Lamb Shoulder with Yogurt Sauce

Slow-roasting was traditionally a community affair. In European villages, bakers made use of their ovens as the fires died down overnight to slow-roast meats for sale. And in the American South, slow-roasting is the foundation of barbecue. Although the method—which lets connective tissue break down and tenderize the meat—is ideal for roasting whole animals and tougher, less expensive cuts, many chefs now slow-roast all kinds of meat, fish, and poultry. Because moisture is drawn to high heat, with low-temperature roasting the moisture remains inside the meat, so you get a uniformly succulent piece of meat, pink throughout with no color deviation except the thin browned ring of a nicely seared crust.

SERVES

LEVEL *of* **DIFFICULTY**

WORTH THE EFFORT

REASONABLE

EASY

SPICE MIX
2 tbsp coriander seeds
2 tbsp fennel seeds
2 tbsp black peppercorns
3 bay leaves

1 boneless lamb shoulder, about 3½ lb/1.6 kg, butterflied and tied by your butcher
Kosher salt
¼ cup/60 g harissa paste (available in better markets)
3 garlic cloves
1 tsp ground cinnamon
¼ cup/60 ml water
½ cup/120 ml extra-virgin olive oil

YOGURT SAUCE
2 cups/480 ml yogurt
¼ cup/60 ml extra-virgin olive oil
2 tbsp fresh lemon juice
2 tbsp finely diced preserved lemon peel*
3 tbsp chopped fresh mint
3 tbsp chopped fresh cilantro
2 tsp ground cumin
Kosher salt →

Preserved lemon peel is available at specialty markets. Dice only the skin, and discard the flesh and any white pith.

1. TO MAKE THE SPICE MIX:
In a small, dry skillet, toast the coriander seeds, fennel seeds, peppercorns, and bay leaves over medium heat until aromatic, 2 to 4 minutes. Immediately slide onto a plate to cool. Set aside.

2. Remove the lamb from the refrigerator and let come to room temperature before cooking, up to 2 hours (this helps the meat cook evenly). Place the lamb on a roasting rack and set the rack on a heavy-duty baking sheet so the roast isn't resting directly on the pan (so the juices pool there and air can circulate on all sides). Thirty minutes before cooking, liberally season the roast with salt.

3. Preheat the oven to 450°F/230°C.

4. Put the toasted spice mix in a blender or small food processor and add the harissa paste, garlic, cinnamon, 1 tbsp salt, and the water and pulse to mix. With the machine running, add the ½ cup/120 ml olive oil and blend just to combine, a few seconds.

5. Rub the lamb all over with the harissa mixture and place in the hot oven to sear for 20 minutes. Remove the lamb from the oven and lower the oven temperature to 225°F/110°C; leave the oven door ajar for 10 minutes to help cool it down. Return the lamb to the oven, close the oven door, and roast until an instant-read thermometer inserted into the thickest part registers 140°F/60°C, 2½ to 3½ hours.

6. WHILE THE LAMB IS ROAST-ING, MAKE THE YOGURT SAUCE: In a small bowl, combine all the sauce ingredients and whisk until well blended. Store, tightly covered, in the refrigerator for up to 2 days.

7. When the roast is done, remove from the oven and let rest for 30 minutes. Transfer to a carving board. Snip off the butcher's twine and carve across the grain on the diagonal into slices about ¼ in/6 mm thick. Serve immediately, passing the sauce at the table.

To feed more people, make two roasts—just be sure to space them about 6 in/15 cm apart in the oven.

SLOW-ROAST

↓

BEFORE slow-roasting the meat in this recipe, you sear it in a hot oven. Some people talk about this blast of heat as "locking in juices." That's a misconception. You sear a roast to develop flavor. Without this step, you won't get any surface browning (related to the combination of carbohydrate molecules and amino acids, known as caramelization), the textural contrast to the sumptuous, tender interior.

SLOW-ROASTING is about temperature; it takes three temperature gauges. Oven thermostats vary in calibration—you can set the temperature, but that doesn't guarantee it will be right. That's why you also need a hardware- or kitchen-store oven thermometer. Preheat the oven for 30 minutes and check the thermometer. If it doesn't match what the oven's set to, adjust the oven accordingly. Then you'll need an instant-read meat thermometer, preferably with a digital probe, to insert into the thickest part of the roast to test doneness. Internal temperature is the only accurate gauge of whether it's ready to eat.

DON'T RUIN a great piece of meat by slicing it too quickly. The fibers of the meat still need time to relax after cooking, letting the natural juices redistribute so they don't pour out when you carve. So wait a half hour (or 10 to 15 minutes for smaller cuts of meat), then remove the butcher's twine and slice.

A SHOULDER ROAST can be rubbed, rolled, and tied the day before, then taken out of the refrigerator to come to room temperature the next day. A slow roast is perfect for a party. As long as you remember to check on it from time to time, once it's in the oven, your work is done and you have plenty of time to set up while the house fills with the incredible aromas of roasting lamb fat, herbs, and garlic.

SANDWICH IDEAS FOR

LEFTOVER LAMB SHOULDER

1. Warm, with Harissa-Yogurt Sauce (see page 130) on flatbread

2. Warm, with olive tapenade and tomato on ciabatta

3. Warm, with mango chutney on naan

4. Warm, with red onion, goat cheese, and fresh mint on crusty bread

Meatballs

Philadelphia is a red-sauce town—what we call "gravy"—but I'm not a big fan of spaghetti and meatballs. I prefer to make a meatball that stands alone, maybe resting on a small base of polenta or some good grilled bread. Nothing that detracts from the meatball itself. This habit of mine is likely rooted in the various Italian regional ways of serving meatballs without pasta, sometimes as a second course, or even the Sicilian *polpettine alla griglia* (grilled meatballs with a touch of lemon) that make me think meatballs are related to the ground-meat kabobs of the Arabs and Greeks who dominated that island for centuries.

In any case, making a tender meatball relies on a few basic principles. First there's *ratio*: about 20 percent of the meat mix should be fat. In my restaurant—and this is a huge benefit of being a pizzeria—I can grind the end nubs of cured meats like prosciutto or sopressata to get fat and flavor at the same time. But at home, I use pancetta or nice smoky bacon. Quality matters because during the low, slow oven cooking, the fat flows out of the meatballs and goes right into the tomato sauce.

Then there's *shape*, and here you want to make sure to get all the air out as you form the meatball. For that I use an old-fashioned trigger ice-cream scoop. Firmly pack the meat into the scoop, pressing down on the flat side with your palm. Then use the spring trigger to release it, and roll it between your flattened palms into a ball. Of course, between the mix and the shaping comes the *filler*, added for texture and to help retain shape. I go really easy—just bread crumbs, salt, and pepper. A meatball should taste like meat.

SERVES

12

*(makes 25 to
30 meatballs)*

LEVEL *of*
DIFFICULTY

WORTH
THE EFFORT

REASONABLE

EASY

MEAT MIX
1 lb/455 g ground beef (80 percent
lean/20 percent fat)
1 lb/455 g ground pork
1 lb/455 g ground veal
1 lb/455 g pancetta or thick-sliced smoky
bacon, finely minced
2 large eggs
⅓ cup/45 g finely grated Parmigiano-
Reggiano
½ yellow onion, finely diced
8 garlic cloves, minced

HERB MIX
¼ cup/15 g minced fresh flat-leaf parsley
2 tbsp chopped fresh oregano
2 tbsp chopped fresh rosemary

⅓ cup/45 g fine dried plain bread crumbs
About ½ cup/120 ml whole milk
Coarse salt and freshly ground black
pepper
Canola oil for frying
About 3 qt/2.8 L tomato sauce, homemade
(see page 95) or good-quality store-
bought, kept warm over low heat
Finely grated Parmigiano-Reggiano
for serving
Warm crusty bread for serving

1. In a large bowl, combine the Meat
Mix with the Herb Mix and knead
the mixture gently with your hands,
like dough; do not overmix.
2. Put the bread crumbs in a medium
bowl. Slowly add the milk, stirring,
just until the mixture has the consistency of wet sand. Immediately add
to the meat mixture, along with 1 tsp
salt and 1½ tsp pepper, and mix
gently until well combined.

3. Heat a small amount of oil in a small
skillet. When the oil is hot—it will
ripple in the pan—pinch off a bit of
meat mixture and fry it in the oil until
browned and cooked through. Remove
with a spoon, taste, and correct the seasoning, if needed. Refrigerate the meat
mixture for about 30 minutes.
4. Preheat the oven to 350°F/180°C.
5. Shape the meatballs, preferably
using an ice-cream scoop (see recipe
introduction). Pour oil into a large
skillet to a depth of about a ¼ in/6 mm
and heat over medium-high heat until
very hot. Working in batches, brown
the meatballs on all sides. As each
batch is finished, transfer to a deep,
ovenproof casserole.
6. When all of the meatballs are
browned, pour in the tomato sauce to
cover. (Don't skimp—they must be
totally submerged.) Place the dish in
the oven and bake until the meatballs
are well done, 1¾ to 2 hours. When
done, they should feel firm to the
touch, or an instant-read thermometer
inserted into the center of the thickest
meatball should register 160°F/71°C.
7. Spoon two or three meatballs per
person onto serving plates, spoon sauce
over, and top with Parmigiano. Pass
the bread when serving.

MEHDI BRUNET-BENKRITLY | FEDORA | *New York, New York*

Côte de Boeuf with Fried Rice

I'm crazy about fried rice. It's like a blank canvas: you can open your fridge and with just a few ingredients make something incredibly flavorful. I traveled in Asia a little, and the best fried rice I ever had was in Vietnam, where they add all kinds of crazy stuff and there are always a lot of crunchy bits on top. Often they'll add off-cuts of meat like chicken hearts, tongue. But I think fried rice with a beautiful côte de boeuf, or rib steak, is tough to beat, because it has a really nice fat cap on it, which replicates some of the richness that they achieve with those other cuts, which aren't so common here.

That's all côte de boeuf is—a cut of the beef rib. It's the same muscle as the rib eye, but higher up, near the shoulder. Very traditional, very French—and very pricey. It's a special cut, for a special meal. The soy butter addition I use at Fedora is borrowed from the French technique of topping steak with *maître d'hôtel* butter, which is simply butter with an added flavor. I use soy sauce, because soy sauce with beef is so good—think of a classic stir-fry.

Don't be intimidated by frying the rice. It's simple—you need a lot of heat, and you need to act quickly. (If it seems at all mysterious, there are plenty of good videos on the Internet.) If you have any leftover tongue or chicken hearts, by all means throw them in. But that's strictly optional.

SERVES

4

LEVEL of DIFFICULTY

WORTH THE EFFORT

REASONABLE

EASY

SOY BUTTER
8 oz/230 g unsalted butter, softened
2 tbsp light soy sauce
Zest of 1 lemon
Freshly ground black pepper

One 32-oz/910-g rib steak
Coarse salt
1 tbsp unsalted butter
1 tbsp canola oil

FRIED RICE
1 tbsp canola oil
2 cups/280 g cooked but still firm sushi rice*

Generous 1 cup/140 g stemmed, brushed clean, and coarsely chopped shiitake mushrooms
1 bunch scallions, white parts chopped and green parts slivered and kept separate
2 large eggs, lightly beaten
2 tbsp light soy sauce
2 tbsp fresh lemon juice
1 tbsp honey
Sriracha sauce

Sea salt
½ lemon
Freshly ground black pepper →

Sushi rice is available at most supermarkets, but in a pinch, stop by a sushi restaurant and pick up a couple orders to go. Whether you make or buy the rice, it can't be over-cooked, or it will get mushy when stir-fried.

1. MAKE THE SOY BUTTER A DAY IN ADVANCE: Combine the butter, soy sauce, and lemon zest in a small bowl. Season with pepper and beat with a wooden spoon until well blended. Place the butter on a piece of plastic wrap and mold into the shape of a sausage. Wrap tightly and refrigerate. (Tightly wrapped, the soy butter will keep in the refrigerator for up to 2 weeks.)

2. Preheat the oven to 375°F/190°C.

3. Generously season the steak with coarse salt. In a large cast-iron skillet over high heat, melt the unsalted butter in the canola oil. When the butter starts to brown and everything's smoking, place the meat in the pan. Don't move it around. When the first side reaches a deep brown color—about 5 minutes—turn and brown the other side, 3 to 4 minutes. Then transfer the pan to the oven and bake for about 10 minutes for medium-rare, or until an instant-read thermometer inserted into the thickest part of the steak registers between 115° and 125°F/46° and 52°C. Transfer to a carving board and let rest while you cook the rice (the internal temperature will rise to between 120° and 130°F/49° and 54°C).

4. TO MAKE THE FRIED RICE: Heat a stainless-steel skillet or wok over high heat until it's very hot, then add the canola oil. Add the rice and work it gently with a wooden spoon for about 1 minute. Add the mushrooms and fry for another minute or two. When all that starts to caramelize, add the white parts of the scallions and fry for 1 minute more, scraping up any browned bits from the bottom of the skillet with the spoon.

5. At this point, you have to be quick and ready: Add the eggs, letting them cook for a moment before breaking them up with the spoon. Pour in the soy sauce, lemon juice, and honey and stir, again scraping the skillet bottom. Once the liquid is absorbed, remove the skillet from the heat. (The rice should stir-fry for 5 to 6 minutes total.) Kick it up a notch with Sriracha to taste, and sprinkle the green parts of the green onions over the top.

6. If the meat has cooled too much, warm it in the oven for 3 minutes. Meanwhile, pile the rice on a platter. Carve the meat, slicing thinly across the grain on a diagonal. Arrange atop the rice. Slice the soy butter into four or five thin disks (reserve the rest for another use) and set on top of the warm meat. Sprinkle a bit of sea salt on the steak. Sprinkle the juice from the lemon half and a grinding of pepper on top of all that. Serve immediately.

Serve the fried rice with sautéed greens— spinach, bok choy, or whatever looks good.

STEAK (DISGUISED AS) SALAD

Buy **2 MONSTER BONELESS SIRLOIN STEAKS** (2 to 2½ lb/910 g to 1.2 kg each and about 2 in/5 cm thick; the butcher will cut them for you) and grill or sear them in a heavy skillet coated with **OIL** (over high heat, 3 to 4 minutes per side with vent on and window open) and finish in 350°F/180°C preheated oven until medium-rare (an instant-read thermometer will register about 130°F/54°C in the thickest part), about 12 minutes. Let the meat cool completely. While the meat is cooling, crank the oven up to 400°F/200°C and roast about **24 SMALL NEW POTATOES** until easily pierced by the tip of a paring knife, 18 to 20 minutes. When cool, halve them. Cut the meat into large cubes. Place the meat and potatoes in a large bowl and drizzle lightly—don't drown them—with a **GOOD VINAIGRETTE** (1 part vinegar to 3 parts oil with a dollop of grainy mustard; or a store-bought creamy garlic will work). Add **2 SEEDED AND DICED RED BELL PEPPERS, 2 SEEDED AND DICED GREEN BELL PEPPERS, 3 DICED CELERY STALKS** (along with as many **CELERY LEAVES** as possible), a **FEW SLIVERED SCALLIONS**, and **SOME CHOPPED FRESH PARSLEY** (if you have it). Toss gently and let the salad sit at room temp for 30 minutes. Now season with **SALT** and **PEPPER** and add more dressing, if needed. (There should not be any vinaigrette pooled in the bottom of the bowl.) Serve with **BIG CHUNKS OF WARM BREAD** smeared with **TANGY BLUE CHEESE. SERVES 16.**

Country Pot Roast

Braising is a two-step technique that works best with economical cuts of meat like chuck, shank, and brisket. The meat is first browned on the stove, covered, and then slowly cooked at a low temperature (either in the oven or on the stove) in a small amount of seasoned liquid so that connective tissue and the meat's own fat melt away to flavor and enrich that cooking liquid, yielding very tender results. Braising is about steam. It requires a pot or dish that's heavy enough to regulate and distribute heat evenly throughout the meat during the cooking process and that can be used on the stove top as well as in the oven. The lid should fit tightly so the steam from the simmering liquid can rise, collect, and condense, and then drip back into the pot to ensure continuous, natural basting.

SERVES

8

LEVEL *of* DIFFICULTY

WORTH THE EFFORT

REASONABLE

EASY

3½ to 4 lb/1.6 to 1.8 kg chuck roast,
    at least 3 in/7.5 cm thick
½ cup/60 g all-purpose flour
1 tbsp onion powder
2 tsp garlic powder
4 garlic cloves, halved lengthwise
Coarse salt and freshly ground black
    pepper
2 tbsp canola oil
6 tbsp/90 g unsalted butter, melted
4 sweet onions such as Vidalia, halved
    from stem to root ends and
    cut crosswise into slices about
    ½ in/12 mm wide
1 lb/455 g button mushrooms, brushed
    clean and sliced
¾ cup/180 ml bourbon
1½ cups/360 ml Madeira or marsala
    or other inexpensive, sweet cooking
    wine (not sherry)
3 cups/720 ml chicken stock
Several sprigs fresh rosemary and
    parsley, tied together with kitchen
    twine
1 to 2 tbsp Dijon mustard (optional)

1. Preheat the oven to 325°F/165°C. While the oven is heating, let the roast come to room temperature.

2. In a small bowl, whisk together the flour, onion powder, and garlic powder. Transfer the seasoned flour to a large, shallow plate or pie pan and set aside.

3. Using a sharp knife, cut eight small slits into veins of fat where you see them on the roast, or into the meat itself, spacing them evenly. Insert the garlic halves into the slits, tucking them in fully so they don't pop out when the roast contracts during cooking. Then, using your hands, generously season with salt and pepper all over, rubbing into the meat. (Don't be shy about the amount of salt you use; the salt draws the juices out of the roast.) Place the roast in the flour mixture, turning to coat it well all over. There will be a good coating of flour on the roast.*

4. Heat the oil in a cast-iron skillet over medium-high heat until it shimmers. Add the butter and cook until the water in the butter boils off and the milk solids sink to the bottom of the pan, about 30 seconds. Wait for the milk solids to boil off, about 30 seconds longer, and then put the roast into the pan to sear. It should sizzle loudly.

5. Lower the heat a bit. After a minute or so, using tongs or a fork, make sure that the roast isn't stuck to the pan and can slide easily, but don't mess with it too much. Let it get a good, dark-brown sear on the first side, about 5 minutes. Do not undercook—gray meat is not seared meat. Turn over and cook the other side the same way. When both sides are browned, remove the roast from the skillet and place on a roasting rack or wire cooling rack.******

6. Raise the heat under the skillet to medium-high. Add the onions to the hot fat. Using a wooden spoon or spatula, stir the onions, scraping up any and all browned bits stuck to the bottom of the pan. Sprinkle with salt and pepper and cook until the onions start to soften, 2 to 3 minutes. Add the mushrooms and stir, seasoning with salt and pepper as you go. Cook, stirring often, until the mushrooms soften and start to release their juices, 4 to 5 minutes. Add the bourbon (careful, it may flame up), stir well, and let boil for 2 minutes. Add the Madeira and bring to a boil again. Let reduce for 5 minutes. (Taste the liquid to make sure all the alcohol has burned off.) Add the chicken stock and bring to a boil. Taste the braising liquid for salt and pepper—too little salt in the broth will make the roast significantly less flavorful, and the dish hinges on a good kick of black pepper balanced against the sweetness of the bourbon and Madeira.

7. If you have a small rack that fits in a Dutch oven, place it in the bottom of the pot. (If you don't, don't worry, but the rack will keep the roast elevated and help prevent scorching.) Set the roast in the pot and tuck the herbs around. Pour the onion mixture over the roast, making sure that the liquid comes only halfway up the sides of the roast. Using the wooden spoon, scrape any mushrooms and onions off the top surface of the roast and into the cooking liquid. Bring the liquid back up just to a simmer—not a full boil, just a slight agitation of the surface and tiny bubbles around the sides of the pot. Place the lid on the pot and put it in the oven. Braise until fork-tender, 3 to 4 hours.

8. Remove the pot from the oven and let the meat rest in the liquid just long enough for the roast to reabsorb its juices before serving, about 15 minutes. And whether it's July or December, you need to offset the deep, dark, undertone flavors of braised beef with a little "brightness" in the form of acidity. I often whisk the Dijon mustard into the liquid. (Or I copy my grandmother and serve chow chow or bread-and-butter pickles on the side.)

9. Transfer the roast to a carving board and slice thinly across the grain on a diagonal. Arrange the slices on a platter. Stir any juices that collected on the board and platter into the cooking liquid. Ladle the cooking liquid into a small pitcher and pass at the table for guests to pour over their servings. Serve immediately.

✳
Ultimately, the melted butter and the flour coating on the roast form a makeshift roux in the oven, designed to slightly thicken the cooking liquid.

✳✳
If you set the hot roast to rest on a flat surface, it will bleed and you'll lose precious liquid.

SANDWICH IDEAS FOR

LEFTOVER POT ROAST

1 Warm, with horseradish mayo on an onion roll

2 Warm, with melted Swiss cheese on an everything bagel

3 Warm, with grainy mustard and pickled hot peppers on pumpernickel

4 Warm, with pickled chow chow on sourdough

Nanny's Brisket with Onions

Unlike many chefs who proclaim, truthfully or not, that they learned to cook as children, holding the apron strings of their grandma, my food experiences growing up were more the result of restaurant experiences than anything else. But there are a few notable and influential exceptions, and among them is my grandmother's brisket. Nanny, as we called her, would break out the brisket for every holiday and family gathering. I always enjoyed it—the falling-apart-tender meat, the oniony flavor. She never seemed to be laboring over it, though. The Carlton 100's still got smoked, and the JELL-O mold with canned mandarin orange segments and Cool Whip always got made on time. In revisiting the recipe many years later, I came to realize the reason: the shortcut of using Lipton Onion Soup Mix. This recipe is a snapshot of a certain time. It shows the intersection of a historically Jewish dish, brisket, with that distinctly American idea of cooking with cans and boxes. The result is simple and delicious.

SERVES

12

LEVEL of DIFFICULTY

WORTH THE EFFORT

REASONABLE

EASY

Brisket is a large cut of meat from the breast or lower chest section that is usually marketed in two smaller cuts. The flat end, called the "first cut," is leaner, while the point cut, referred to as the "deckle cut," has more fat and so is a bit more flavorful.

One 10-lb/4.5-kg first-cut brisket (the leaner end)*
Four 1-oz/30-g pouches Lipton Onion Soup Mix
Freshly ground black pepper
¼ cup/60 g Dijon mustard
4 large yellow onions, thinly sliced
4 garlic cloves, chopped

1. Season the brisket on all sides with the soup mix and a few grinds of pepper. Place the brisket in a roasting pan and spread the mustard over the top and sides. Let the meat rest.

2. Preheat the oven to 325°F/165°C.

3. When the oven is ready, completely cover the surface of the brisket with the onions and garlic. Pour water into the roasting pan until it comes halfway up the sides of the brisket, then cover the pan tightly with aluminum foil—two sheets vertically (overlapping and sealed) and two horizontally (overlapping and sealed) so no steam can escape. Roast until

tender, 5 to 6 hours. To test for doneness, don't unwrap the pan. Just insert a metal skewer through the foil, making sure the meat is tender enough to be easily pierced.

4. Transfer the brisket to a carving board and let rest for about 1 hour. To carve, slice the meat across the grain on the diagonal. Serve dressed with the juices and onions from the pot.

TIP

The brisket can be made a day ahead and reheated. It is delicious served with boiled potatoes and braised cabbage.

MICHAEL SYMON | LOLA | *Cleveland, Ohio*

Midwestern Matambre

There's a lot of story behind this beast. It has roots in the Argentine *matambre*, or "hunger killer," and my version accomplishes the same. But I'm from Cleveland, and so I go big on my local flavor. Instead of flank steak, I use brisket (because it tenderizes during the braise) with an earthy filling of what grows hardy in the Great Lakes region, plus a healthy dose of kielbasa, all served up on a hot cabbage slaw thickened by mustard and horseradish. Although you'll learn to switch out the ingredients depending upon your own tastes, there are two things to consider: You need a piece of meat cut from the widest part of the entire brisket, then butterflied open with the grain (splayed open like a book with a binding-like seam) and lightly pounded. The ultimate goal is a wide rectangle of meat shaped like a flag, not a belt. And to get a uniform, tight cylinder of meat that looks better and cooks evenly, the carrot, parsnip, and kielbasa should be cut into matchstick shapes (¼ by ¼ in/6 by 6 mm wide and 2 in/5 cm long, or as close as you can get) called *batonnet*. Then it goes together quickly—just roll and rock.

SERVES

6

(but easily multiplied)

LEVEL *of* DIFFICULTY

WORTH THE EFFORT

REASONABLE

EASY

One 1¾-lb/800-g brisket, butterflied (split horizontally lengthwise but still in one piece, and opened like a book) and lightly pounded
Coarse salt and freshly ground pepper
8 oz/230 g kale, stemmed (including tough center spines)
1 large parsnip and 1 large carrot, peeled and cut into matchsticks (or as uniformly as you can; see recipe introduction)
8 oz/230 g kielbasa, cut into the same shape as the parsnip and carrot

About ¼ cup/60 ml canola oil, or more as needed*

1 lb/455 g slab bacon (not too smoky), thickly sliced and cut into lardons (small strips)
2 lb/910 g white cabbage, cored and cut into slices about ¼ in/6 mm thick
2 garlic cloves, minced
2 white onions, halved lengthwise and cut crosswise into slices ¼ in/6 mm thick
1 tsp red pepper flakes
One 12-oz/360-ml bottle dark beer (I use La Rossa)
2 bay leaves
¼ cup/60 g grainy mustard
Prepared white horseradish (I like Gold's) →

Be generous with the oil. You need enough oil to carry the heat to the meat, and most of it is going to end up in splatters on the stove, anyway.

1. As far in advance as you can, even the night before, season the meat with salt and pepper, cover with plastic wrap, and refrigerate.

2. Preheat the oven to 350°F/180°C. Take the meat out of the refrigerator to take the chill off.

3. Have ready a large bowl of ice water. Bring a large pot of water to a boil. Immerse the kale in the boiling water until the leaves deepen slightly in color, about 45 seconds. Using tongs, remove the kale from the pot, letting the excess cooking water drain, and plunge immediately into the bowl of ice water. When cool, drain in a colander and squeeze dry.

4. Lay the meat, seam-side down, on a work surface. Leaving about ½ in/ 12 mm all around the edges, arrange the kale over the meat and, working in horizontal sections, lay the parsnip, carrot, and kielbasa over the leaves (a band of carrot across the top third, a band of kielbasa in the middle, and a band of parsnip along the bottom, for example, like a flag). Roll the meat horizontally, from bottom to top, as tightly as you can. Tie with kitchen twine about every 1½ in/4 cm or so to secure the roll.

5. Place a large, flameproof roasting pan (for example, 12 in/30.5 cm wide and 18 in/46 cm long) on two burners on the stove top. Add the oil and heat over high heat. When the oil is shimmering hot, add the meat and, using tongs to rotate, quickly sear on all sides to prevent the cut from curling. Then do a longer sear, turning as needed, to get it crusty brown on all sides.

6. Remove the meat from the pan and set aside on a platter. Add the bacon to the hot pan, turn the heat to medium, and cook until the fat is rendered, about 8 minutes. Add the cabbage, garlic, onions, red pepper flakes, beer, and bay leaves and let the liquid come to a simmer, wilting the cabbage a bit. Return the meat and any juices from the platter to the roasting pan and cover securely with a double thickness of aluminum foil, making sure all the edges are sealed.

7. Place the pan in the oven and roast until the meat is tender, about 2 hours. To test for doneness, insert a metal skewer through the foil (so the cooking steam doesn't escape if the roast isn't ready). The skewer will go into the meat with no resistance when done. Remove the meat from the oven, transfer to a carving board, and let rest for about 10 minutes. Place the pan on two burners again over medium heat. Add the mustard, stirring to incorporate. Add the horseradish, 1 tsp at a time, to taste. Carve the rolled roast against the grain into six pieces. Serve immediately with the cabbage, drizzled with the pan sauce.

SANDWICH IDEAS FOR
LEFTOVER MATAMBRE

1 Sliced thinly, on garlic toast

2 Sliced thinly, with dressed baby spinach and shaved carrot on a hoagie roll

3 Sliced thinly, with sliced hard-boiled eggs and roasted peppers on a kaiser roll

4 Sliced thinly, with pesto on focaccia

BE A GOOD GUEST

There comes a time in every man's life when an invitation to dine means more than a pizza box and a pop-top. And whether your crossover moment arrives via phone, text, e-vite, or—imagine this—mail, a prompt response is the first sign of a good guest. Here's how to leave your mark on the rest of the evening.

1

BE ON TIME

Your invitation will tell you what time to arrive, and that's exactly when your host expects to see you. Ten minutes late is acceptable, but ten minutes in the other direction won't work. You'd be surprised by the number of last-minute adjustments taking place right before guests arrive, and in many of these situations, the early bird actually becomes the worm.

2

DON'T BRING ANYTHING

When you are invited to a formal dinner party, rest assured that your hosts have already planned (and paid) for everything they need, including wine, dessert, and particularly flowers. Taking an expensive vase from a hard-to-reach cupboard makes cleaning, cutting, and arranging a bunch of guest-gift flowers an imposition. If you insist on believing your mother about never arriving empty-handed, a box of hand-packed boutique chocolates requires no maintenance and is still considered a luxury, regardless of income bracket.

ENGAGE

At smaller parties, a savvy host will make introductions that include a little biographical information about each guest to encourage conversation. At larger gatherings, you can use the same technique: "Hi, I'm John Smith" is a dead end, but "I'm John Smith, and I knew Mike before he became a big hedge-fund guy" can lead somewhere. Just remember that a good conversation consists of talking *and* listening, even when you consider yourself the most interesting person in the room.

NO MATTER WHAT THEY SAY, SPECIAL ORDERS *DO* UPSET HOSTS

Legitimate food imperatives are the hosts' problem. Explain them when you accept the invitation. Food issues of your own choosing (like you eat carbs only on alternate Tuesdays) are your problem. Keep them to yourself.

MAKE A GRACEFUL AND TIMELY EXIT

During a seated dinner party, the phrase "coffee in the living room" is the uptown equivalent of "last call." At cocktail parties, it's time to say good-night when the hosts station themselves near the door. They want you to use it.

GIVE THANKS

Always send a handwritten thank-you note. Depending on your relationship with the hosts, small gifts (like books or music) are entirely appropriate. In more formal situations, you may choose to send flowers. But don't thank a four-star meal with an arrangement that screams McFlowers. Not unless you want your next dinner invitation to include a drive-through window.

JEFF McINNIS | **YARDBIRD** | *Miami Beach, Florida*

Doritos Nachos

I have to give credit where it's due: One night at the restaurant, my sous chef, CJ, invented this dish with a bag of Blazin' Buffalo & Ranch Doritos he had in his backpack. But I've made it at home many times since. It's pretty common for us to have a few barbecued ribs left on the grill, sitting in sauce, and we always have fried chicken. But you can use pulled pork, roast chicken, or whatever leftovers you have—it's not an exact science. The most important thing is the assembly: The meat-and-cheese party happens on top, so spread the chips evenly on the pan, then distribute the toppings evenly so that everyone gets their fair share. And I scatter an extra ring of cheese directly on the pan, around the perimeter, so that it gets nice and hard and crispy.

If it's late and you're hungry, carry the entire pan into the living room and set it on a towel on the coffee table. (Warning from personal experience: Do not put the hot pan on the couch.) Eat with your hands and don't forget to pull off the crispy cheese pieces stuck to the pan.

SERVES

4

LEVEL of DIFFICULTY

WORTH THE EFFORT

REASONABLE

EASY

One 11½-oz/325-g bag Doritos, your favorite flavor (eat some while you're waiting)

About 3 cups/1.8 kg shredded mixed cooked meat, such as pork and chicken

About 2 cups/225 g shredded Cheddar cheese (or Muenster or pepper Jack, whatever you have)

¼ cup/65 g canned black beans (optional)

Barbecue sauce, homemade or your favorite bottled

Optional toppings: sour cream, salsa, guacamole, Sriracha sauce, Tabasco sauce

1. Preheat the oven to 350°F/180°C.

2. Spread the chips on a 13-by-15-in/33-by-38-cm rimmed baking sheet in a somewhat even layer. Evenly distribute the shredded meat over the top. Top evenly with the cheese, putting a little extra directly on the pan around the perimeter of the nachos. Sprinkle the beans (if using) over the top.

3. Bake until the cheese is melted and the nachos are crisply browned, about 12 minutes. Remove from the oven and drizzle lightly with the barbecue sauce. Serve hot, with the toppings of your choice.

The Late-Night Pantry

*If eating after midnight is a rare occasion at your house, a frozen pizza works.
But for the late-night habitué who needs more rewarding options, it takes some
judicious stockpiling. The best after-hours pantry is ruled by two criteria: flexibility
(gotta have lots of uses) and perishability (gotta last at least a week).*

↓

PICKLES

Sandwiches are the key to late night and pickles are the key to great sandwiches, so buy the best. Gordy's have a slow build of heat that delivers flavor in the backseat instead of mowing you down on the first bite.

SALAMI

Presliced meat is for school lunches. What you need is a nightstick from Olympic Provisions; a slim cylinder of all-pork salami intensified by an injection of good-quality fat.

CHOCOLATE

If there's anything coffee roasters understand, it's blending, and that's why La Colombe's milk chocolate is just as nuanced as its Turkish dark chocolate. A small piece of either does the trick—this is chocolate *food*.

PEANUT BUTTER

The perfect late-night food, requiring nothing more than a twist of the lid and your finger. Koeze, made with Virginia peanuts, is soft and swirly, with just the right amount of salt.

FROZEN WAFFLES

Because they make you feel like a kid. Because you can put ice cream on them, or peanut butter. And because it's almost morning anyway.

POTATO CHIPS

Smashed into sandwiches, potato chips are the thinking man's lettuce. Once a bag is open, it will rarely last long enough to get stale.

SARA LEE POUND CAKE

Devotees can attest to the joy of eating this cold from the fridge, when it's so dense you can see your teeth marks. The more patient toast it.

CHOCOLATE– PEANUT BUTTER ICE CREAM

Let it soften and stir the hell out of it. Homemade soft-serve.

HOT DOGS

For sandwiches, scrambling into eggs, or bulking up canned soups and beans. Niman Ranch is the best widely available brand.

Hot-Pepper Wings with Cilantro Sour Cream

Every chef has his treats. By that I mean bits and pieces from things you're working on—crusty little cake trimmings, ends from a brisket, collars from a salmon, scraps. But they're snacks to me, and I eat them right off the cutting board—maybe too much. Sometimes, when they are in a large quantity, like chicken wings, they end up in the "family meal." As a chef, this is the best time of my day. The kitchen crew has been playing around with the new dishes, the wait staff is gathering, and we all sit down and eat together. It's like that backstage feeling before the curtain goes up; we're all ready to rock and roll. The kitchen crew takes turns cooking, and it's usually something straightforward like meat loaf, or these wings.

It didn't take long before hot-pepper wings were the back-of-the-house fave at Dahlia. But I couldn't find a spot for them on the menu; as good as they are, they just didn't fit the fine-dining vibe. It took opening the Palace Kitchen, a place with an applewood grill, the right-style menu, and a late-night atmosphere, before the best wings in Seattle found a home in the front of the house as well. Get yourself some he-man-size chunkers (maybe four to six per 1 lb/455 g), grill or broil them intact, and eat the tips—all that skin and cartilage is delicious.

SERVES

LEVEL *of* **DIFFICULTY**

WORTH THE EFFORT

REASONABLE

EASY

MARINADE

2 cups/480 ml soy sauce

1 cup/240 g Dijon mustard

1 cup/240 ml water

¾ cup/180 ml Tabasco sauce

8 garlic cloves, chopped

2 tbsp chopped fresh flat-leaf parsley

2 tsp chopped fresh thyme

2 tsp chopped fresh sage

2 tsp chopped fresh rosemary

18 whole chicken wings

CILANTRO SOUR CREAM

½ cup/120 ml sour cream

2 tbsp heavy cream

2 tsp chopped fresh cilantro

Kosher or coarse salt and freshly
ground black pepper

1. TO MAKE THE MARINADE: In a large bowl, whisk together the marinade ingredients. Reserve ½ cup/120 ml of the marinade for basting.

2. Add the wings to the bowl with the marinade, cover, and refrigerate for at least 1 hour or up to overnight. Turn occasionally to make sure the wings are thoroughly marinated.

3. *GRILL METHOD:* Build a medium-hot fire in a charcoal grill or preheat a gas grill to medium. Let the coals burn down a bit. Remove the wings from the marinade. (Discard the marinade.) Grill the wings over medium-low coals, turning often and moving to cooler areas as needed, until the wings are cooked through, about 15 minutes. You want the wings to cook slowly so they cook thoroughly before the glaze burns. While grilling, heat the reserved marinade in a saucepan and baste the wings a few times while they cook. Cut into a wing to make sure no pink remains near the bone, then remove from the heat.

BROILER METHOD: Preheat the broiler. Remove the wings from the marinade. (Discard the marinade.) Put wings in a broiler pan and slip under the broiler, about 4 in/10 cm from the heat source, and broil for about 10 minutes per side. (If your broiler has a low setting, use that, otherwise watch carefully so the glaze doesn't burn.)

4. Meanwhile, heat the reserved marinade in a saucepan and baste the wings a few times while cooking. Cut into a wing to make sure there is no pink remaining near the bone, then remove from the heat.

5. TO MAKE THE CILANTRO SOUR CREAM: In a small bowl, whisk together the sour cream, heavy cream, and cilantro. Season with salt and pepper.

6. Transfer the wings to a platter and drizzle with 1 tsp of warm reserved marinade. Don't use more than a drizzle; it's really strong. Serve whatever is left on the side for heat lovers. Serve the wings, passing the cilantro sour cream at the table.

Caution: Never use a "raw" marinade—any marinade that has had raw meat in it—to finish a dish. That's why we set some aside in this recipe.

EXTREMELY EASY RECIPE

THE STOMLET *(Steam + Omelette)*

In an 8-in/20-cm skillet that has a lid, melt about **2 TSP BUTTER** over medium-low heat, swirling the pan until the surface of the skillet is covered. Crack in **2 LARGE EGGS**, gently swirling the pan so that the whites spread out and completely cover the surface. (Break the yolks if you like harder eggs.) Cook only until the whites and yolks begin to set, about 3 minutes. Gently add **A THIN SLICE EACH OF HAM AND CHEESE** over the top of the eggs, sprinkle with a **PINCH OF PIMENT D'ESPELETTE SMOKED PAPRIKA**, cover with a lid, and cook until the cheese melts into a smooth dome, about another 2 minutes. If you have **ARUGULA**, add a handful and replace the lid, letting the greens steam and soften slightly, about 90 seconds. Transfer to a plate, or fold in half and layer into a toasted roll for a breakfast sandwich. **SERVES 1** *(multiply for as many as you are willing to make).*

JONATHAN BENNO | LINCOLN RISTORANTE | *New York, New York*

Braised-Sausage Sandwiches

I am a chef and my wife's a chef. When we finally get home, what we're hungry for is more about a long day at work than a long night out on the town. Because we live near one of New York's best old-school Italian butchers, we always have some sausage on hand, which always provides late-night comfort. Cooking on the fly is about convenience, satisfaction, and substance, so I like to braise the sausage in tomato sauce. It's quick and also gets a lot of flavor into the sauce with no extra work. Sometimes we eat it with pasta right then and there, or we use some to make this deeply rewarding sandwich, layered onto a solid crusty roll that has good absorbing power. Whether you call it a grinder, a sub, or a hero, this sandwich always tastes good in the middle of the night.

SERVES

2

(make as many as you like)

LEVEL of DIFFICULTY

WORTH THE EFFORT

REASONABLE

EASY

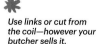

Use links or cut from the coil—however your butcher sells it.

2 sandwich-size pieces Italian sausage*
4 cups/960 ml tomato sauce, home-made (see page 95) or good-quality store-bought brought to a simmer and kept warm
2 long sandwich rolls, split
Thinly sliced fresh mozzarella and freshly grated Parmesan cheese

1. Split each piece of sausage lengthwise, splaying it open like a book. (Don't slice all the way through.) Using a lightly oiled cast-iron or other deep, heavy skillet, brown the sausage on both sides, about 3 minutes per side. Cover with warm tomato sauce, turn the heat to low, and simmer, uncovered, on the stove top until the sausage is cooked through, about 20 minutes.

2. Preheat the broiler.

3. Transfer the sausage to the bottom halves of the rolls, spooning extra sauce over the top. Place the top halves of the rolls under the broiler until lightly toasted, about 60 seconds. Transfer the toasted tops to the center of a double-thickness of aluminum foil, cover with overlapping slices of mozzarella, sprinkle with Parmesan, and return to the broiler until the cheese melts, 2 minutes tops. Place cheese-side down on top of each sausage half. Press lightly to close and serve.

TIP

Once the remaining sauce has cooled, store it, tightly covered, in the refrigerator for up to 1 week and use to sauce pasta on another night.

SEARED-DOG MUFFINS WITH GREEN CHILES AND CHEDDAR

Split 2 **WHOLE-WHEAT ENGLISH MUFFINS** and toast the cut sides under a hot broiler. Lightly oil an 8-in/20-cm cast-iron skillet over medium-high heat. Split a **HOT DOG** lengthwise (don't cut all the way through), splaying it open like a book, then cut in half horizontally. Place cut-side down in the skillet and top with an empty teakettle or a small pan. Brown the dog well, flip, and brown the other sides, maybe 4 minutes total. Arrange each hot dog half on one muffin bottom. Place **SOME SHREDDED OR SLICED CHEDDAR CHEESE** on the other half, top with a **SPOONFUL OF CHOPPED GREEN CHILES**, and return to broiler until the cheese melts, 2 minutes tops. Place cheese-side down on the hot dogs and press to close before serving. SERVES 2.

LEFTOVER CHICKEN SANDWICH

Ashley Christensen, of Poole's Downtown Diner in Raleigh, North Carolina, has just the cure for late night hunger pangs. When a hungry man knocks on your door, he wants an experience he can wrap his hands around. Being single, I often have a leftover half of a roast chicken in the fridge, so this is what I do: Strip **ALL THE MEAT FROM A LEFTOVER CHICKEN** (store-bought rotisserie bird is okay), keeping the skin on. In a cast-iron skillet, cook **4 STRIPS OF BACON** until crispy, then transfer it to paper towels to drain. Add a sprig of **FRESH ROSEMARY** and **A CRUSHED GARLIC CLOVE** to the bacon fat, then transfer the chicken, skin-side down, to the skillet. Baste with the warm bacon fat. Turn and repeat, flavoring and crisping the meat. Meanwhile, preheat the broiler. Remove the chicken from the skillet and put a thin slice of **JARLSBERG CHEESE** on top, which will turn slightly translucent. Split an excellent **BAGUETTE** and toast it under the broiler to the point that it almost cuts the roof of your mouth. Coat the cut sides with **DIJON-MUSTARD-SPIKED MAYO** (Duke's if you're in the South). Fire the cast-iron back up (throw away the garlic clove and rosemary) and fry an **EGG** in the garlicky bacon drippings, cooking a pinch beyond over easy; we'll call it "over easier." Stacking order: coated baguette bottom, a few **SALT-AND-PEPPER-SEASONED TOMATO SLICES**, chicken-cheese packet, fried egg, handful of peppery **ARUGULA**, bacon. Close up the baguette, crushing it down to the point of maneuverability to serve. SERVES 1 *(multiply for as many as you are willing to make)*.

Andouille–French Bread Pizza

I haven't met too many people who don't like hot sausage with melted cheese all over it. This recipe packs a wallop using just a few ingredients—a couple fistfuls of white Cheddar, some good sausage, and pickled jalapeños. We pickle our own jalapeños for this recipe, which we highly recommend—they're crunchy and have a lot more heat than the limp, squishy, jarred varieties found in the supermarket. Even better, you'll end up with a nice spicy vinegar that you can later add to greens, gumbo, or game-day Bloody Marys.

SERVES

LEVEL *of* DIFFICULTY

WORTH THE EFFORT

REASONABLE

EASY

Two 18-in/46-cm loaves good French bread, split in half
1 tbsp vegetable oil
2 lb/910 g andouille sausage, cut into small pieces
1 large yellow onion, chopped
1 cup/240 ml beer
6 cups/300 g shredded white Cheddar cheese
Freshly ground black pepper
3 to 4 cups/360 to 480 g sliced pickled jalapeños, preferably homemade (see page 183)

1. Preheat the oven to 350°F/180°C.
2. Place the bread halves on a baking sheet and toast in the oven for 10 minutes, or until the cut sides are lightly toasted. Remove from the oven and set aside.

3. Heat the oil in a heavy-bottomed sauté pan or cast-iron skillet over medium-high heat. Add the sausage pieces and onion and cook until lightly browned, about 5 minutes. Add the beer (or, you know, just pour some of the beer you're already drinking into the mixture). Let the liquid cook down for about 5 minutes.
4. Spread the cooked sausage mixture over the toasted bread and sprinkle the cheese on top. Raise the oven temperature to 400°F/200°C. Return the pizzas to the oven and cook for 5 to 7 minutes, or until the cheese is bubbling. Grind some pepper on top and garnish with the jalapeños. Cut into generous hunks and serve.

Penne con Ragù di Mortadella

When I get home from work, I go straight to the fridge. Typically my fit Italian wife bans carbs from the cupboard, which doesn't give me anxiety considering I'm surrounded by bread and pasta all day. But when it's up to me, I gravitate toward the one ingredient I always have on hand: Mortadella, an Italian cold-cut staple that's basically a better version of American bologna. Mortadella is king in the White household. Then, depending on how much time and energy I have, I decide what to do with it. On many nights that means a sloppy bowl of pasta with *mortadella ragù*. It's a quick sauce, and the only trick comes in adding the egg to the hot pasta—you just have to be sure it doesn't overcook. I eat this rich goodness in a big plastic Chinese bowl and indulge using chopsticks while watching late-night reruns of *Diners, Drive-ins and Dives*.

SERVES

10

LEVEL *of* **DIFFICULTY**

WORTH THE EFFORT

REASONABLE

EASY

✳
The fancy name for this is chiffonade.

2 lb/910 g dried penne
5 tbsp/70 g unsalted butter
1½ lb/680 g thinly sliced mortadella, rolled and thinly cut on the diagonal*
4 cups/960 ml heavy cream, plus more if needed
Pinch of freshly grated nutmeg
4 egg yolks
Freshly ground black pepper
Coarse salt
1½ cups/175 g freshly grated Parmigiano-Reggiano

1. Bring a pot of salted water to a boil. Add the pasta to the boiling water and cook until almost al dente, about 10 minutes. Reserve 1 cup/240 ml of the cooking liquid, then strain the pasta in a colander set in the sink.

2. In a large Dutch oven, melt the butter over medium-low heat until it begins to foam. Add the mortadella and warm until the fat becomes translucent, about 4 minutes. Add the cream and the nutmeg, and bring to a simmer for 1 to 2 minutes. Remove from the heat.

3. Once the sauce cools a bit, add the pasta and stir to combine. (If it won't all fit, transfer the sauce to a large bowl and then add the pasta.) Make a small well on top of the penne. Add the egg yolks and a grind of pepper, and stir rapidly with the back of a wooden spoon to incorporate the egg into the sauce. (This is called tempering, which ensures that the egg doesn't overcook.) Season with salt. Add the cheese and toss. Eat immediately.

SHANE SOLOMON | **PIZZERIA STELLA** | *Philadelphia, Pennsylvania*

Spaghetti with Butter and Parm

This dish is not about coating spaghetti with sauce. It's about incorporating the two—letting the starch from the pasta enrich the sauce and the sauce soak into the pasta—by building a layered skillet sauce and finishing the cooking of the spaghetti right there in the same pan.

SERVES

2

LEVEL *of* **DIFFICULTY**

WORTH THE EFFORT

REASONABLE

EASY

½ lb/230 g dried spaghetti
3 tbsp extra-virgin olive oil, plus more for drizzling (taste the oil beforehand; you want an oil that tastes really good on its own)
1 or 2 garlic cloves, thinly sliced
Pinch of red pepper flakes
Freshly ground black pepper
1 tbsp unsalted butter, softened
¼ cup/30 g freshly grated Parmesan cheese, plus more for garnish
Chopped fresh flat-leaf parsley for garnish

1. Bring a large pot of abundantly salted water (imagine you're creating ocean water) to a boil. Add the pasta to the boiling water and cook until al dente—still firm to the tooth without being floury—about 7 minutes. (Use tongs to pull a strand out and taste it.)

2. While the pasta is cooking, in a 9-in/23-cm skillet, heat the olive oil over medium heat. Add the garlic and cook gently ("sweating" in the shallow pool of oil). Stir in the red pepper flakes. The goal is to release the flavor of the garlic without browning it. As soon as you get a whiff of garlic, pull the skillet off the heat.

3. When the pasta is done, use tongs to transfer it directly into the warm skillet; reserve the cooking water. Return the skillet to medium heat and stir well to coat the pasta with the infused oil.

4. Now begin adding the warm reserved pasta cooking water while you shake the pan back and forth—maybe a ¼ cup/60 ml at a time, only enough to keep the pasta moving. Continue to toss and stir the pasta, adding cooking water as needed, and let the noodles finish cooking in the skillet sauce. (Over time, you'll learn when the spaghetti "sounds right." As you shake the pan back and forth, flipping the pasta over on itself, the noodles should slap the pan with a *plop*, signifying that you have a heavy, slick sauce. When the pasta is too dry, it won't make this sound.)

5. Season with pepper (as much as you would use on a salad), add the butter, and keep the pan moving. When the noodles are slick with sauce, add the Parmesan (or a small handful, if you're not measuring) and a bit more olive oil (maybe 2 tbsp). Twirl the noodles onto a platter or individual plates. Sprinkle with more Parmesan and the parsley, and serve immediately.

Spaghetti Carbonara

The black pepper needs to be ground at the moment you add it, because when it comes into contact with oxygen it will oxidize and instantly lose flavor. It's a big part of the flavor in this simple dish.

SERVES

4

(as an appetizer or light lunch)

LEVEL *of* DIFFICULTY

WORTH THE EFFORT

REASONABLE

EASY

3 tbsp sea salt
1 lb/455 g spaghetti
6 oz/170 g guanciale, cut into strips the length of a toothpick and ⅛ in/ 4 mm thick*
4 egg yolks
8 tbsp/60 g freshly grated pecorino romano cheese
Freshly ground black pepper

1. Bring a large pot of water to a boil. Stir in the sea salt and add the spaghetti. Move the spaghetti strands around with a long fork so that they don't stick together during the first minute of cooking.

2. Once the spaghetti is cooking, place the guanciale in a sauté pan over low heat to melt the fat, then raise the heat to medium to get nice crisp pieces. Remove from the heat and set aside.

3. In a large bowl, whisk the egg yolks along with 2 tbsp of the cheese and 1 tsp freshly ground pepper.

4. Now comes the simplest but most difficult part: Just when the spaghetti breaks under your teeth without any white streak inside (al dente), it's done—start tasting it when it has been cooking for 3 minutes less than the package instructions say. Using tongs, remove the pasta from the hot water, place it directly in the bowl with the yolk mixture, and toss, adding a little of the cooking water 1 tbsp at a time, just enough to form a creamy sauce. The eggs need to be dense but not scrambled, with the same texture as cream. (If the eggs scramble on the pasta, throw the whole thing away and start over.)

5. Stir in 2 tbsp of the cheese and half of the guanciale. (I add the egg mixture before the guanciale because the fat of the guanciale prevents the eggs from perfectly coating the spaghetti.) Sprinkle a serving platter with another 2 tbsp pecorino, then place the spaghetti in the center and scatter the remaining guanciale on top. Finish with the remaining pecorino and serve immediately.

Guanciale is cured pork cheek. It carries the best-tasting fat.

Anytime Reliables

Vinaigrette

You really only need one viniagrette recipe. This is the one. Memorize it.

SERVES

LEVEL *of* DIFFICULTY

WORTH THE EFFORT

REASONABLE

EASY

1 tbsp Dijon mustard
1 tbsp sherry vinegar
1 tbsp minced fresh tarragon
¼ tsp fine sea salt
⅛ tsp freshly ground black pepper
1¼ cups/300 ml canola or
    safflower oil

1. In a small bowl, combine the mustard, vinegar, tarragon, salt, and pepper. Whisk together until well blended. While whisking continuously, slowly pour in the oil to form a thick emulsion.

2. Store the vinaigrette in the refrigerator in a glass jar with a tight-fitting lid for up to 1 month, shaking well before using.

The Sauce for Every Steak

This is Chicago Cut's signature steak sauce.

SERVES

25+

(makes enough for 28 steaks)

LEVEL *of* **DIFFICULTY**

WORTH THE EFFORT

REASONABLE

EASY

6 cups/1.4 L ketchup
1 tbsp dark brown sugar
1 tbsp light brown sugar
1½ tsp honey
½ tsp Tabasco sauce
¼ tsp white wine vinegar
¼ tsp ground cumin
¼ tsp dried oregano
¼ tsp Hungarian paprika
¼ tsp onion salt
¼ tsp garlic salt
¼ tsp freshly ground
    black pepper
¼ tsp white pepper
¼ tsp red pepper flakes
1 cup/240 ml Lea & Perrins
    Worcestershire sauce
1 tbsp freshly grated
    horseradish (optional)

1. Combine all of the ingredients in a large saucepan and bring to a boil. Turn the heat to low and simmer for 5 minutes, stirring. Remove from the heat and let cool completely.

2. Transfer the sauce to a large glass jar with a tight-fitting lid and close tightly. The sauce can be refrigerated for months (almost forever)—which is good, because this makes about 2 qt/2 L and once you've had it, you'll always want it on hand.

| LAURENT MANRIQUE | MILLESIME | *New York, New York* |

The Sauce for Every Fish (*Sauce Vierge*)

This sauce, called "virgin" because it's uncooked, works on any fish, any style.

SERVES

4

LEVEL *of* **DIFFICULTY**

WORTH THE EFFORT

REASONABLE

EASY

½ cup/120 ml extra-virgin olive oil
1 ripe tomato, cut into small dice
1 tbsp finely chopped sweet onion,
   such as Vidalia
1 tbsp small (nonpareil) capers,
   drained
1 tbsp finely chopped black olives,
   preferably Moroccan
Pulp of ¼ lemon, diced
2 tbsp finely chopped fresh basil
1 tbsp finely chopped fresh tarragon
1 tbsp finely chopped fresh chives
2 tbsp toasted pine nuts* (optional)

Combine all of the ingredients in a bowl 15 minutes before serving so the flavors meld.

In a small, dry pan over medium heat, toast the pine nuts until just fragrant, less than a minute. Stand by the stove. You don't want to burn them.

What Goes with What

THOMAS KELLER

WE ARE FIRST introduced to the way things taste as kids, by our parents. We learn what tastes good together—to us. Peanut butter and jelly. But then when we went to a friend's house for dinner, the experience gave us a different reference point. They ate different foods. The house smelled different. They used a different kind of peanut butter. It was bizarre—and your house seemed just as bizarre to your friend when he came over.

Still, peanut butter and jelly works in any house, pretty much no matter what brands you use. The globby, sweet jelly contrasts with the thick, salty peanut butter, and both are set off by the soft chew of the bread. Foods have what we call flavor profiles, which are kind of like classifications of how they taste. People develop different tastes depending on their cultural or even economic background—and the habits of their parents or whoever fed them as children—but some combinations just work.

There are just a few main flavor profiles: sweet, salty, bitter—and, of course, fat. And then you have factors like spiciness, acidity, and texture to play with. Texture is important because it sets off the ingredients against one another in a satisfying way—that's why there are croutons on salads, and it's why I eat my scrambled eggs with crunchy Ak-Mak crackers. Salt and acidity are the only components that actually enhance flavors. When you're putting together any dish—whether it's a dish at the French Laundry or a midnight snack in your kitchen—all you have to do is keep those ideas in mind and start pairing ingredients with different flavor profiles to see if they taste good. To you. Here are six winners to start with.

SWEET AND SOUR

Strawberries with a drizzle of balsamic vinegar. You see it on dessert menus and while it might be surprising, is it such a leap? In China, it's sweet-and-sour soup. Or think of a classic vinaigrette—sweet and sour are the dominant flavors. I've always loved the combination of pineapple and lime, which is sweet and acid.

FAT AND ANYTHING

Anything added to fat can give you a wonderful feeling. It explodes when you add salt, which is why the edges of steak are always so delicious if they've been seasoned amply before cooking. Or sweet and fat—think of fried plantains.

SWEET AND SALT

Prosciutto wrapped around cantaloupe is a classic snack. Ever sprinkle some really good salt on a particularly sugary honeydew melon? Also consider traditional *bagna cauda*, the Italian dip that combines super-salty anchovies with a different kind of sweetness: garlic.

SOUR AND BOWL FOOD

You can add vinegar to almost any dish you'd eat in a bowl—risotto, stew, soup. Food eaten from bowls tends to be rich. Add a few drops of sherry vinegar, red wine vinegar, malt vinegar, balsamic, or whatever you have, and it enhances everything that's in the pot.

SPICY AND SWEET

Ginger snaps with peanut butter is one of the all-time great snacks because spicy and sweet go together so well. Plus, you have the textural contrast of creamy and crunchy, assuming you use the crunchy cookies, not the soft ones. Which you always should.

POTATOES AND ANYTHING

We all love silky, creamy, buttery mashed potatoes. They taste like our childhoods. But they have no textural contrast and no contrasting flavors. So you can add extreme opposites like bits of bacon and fried shallots, or sharp cheese, and they are transformed.

Oil: A Tutorial

Oil is a vehicle, used during cooking to transfer heat or after cooking to impart flavor (the drizzle). But no oil can do both. That's why some oils undergo commercial processing to remove flavorful, fragrant sediments. This clarifies the oil and raises the smoke point (the temperature at which an oil stops delivering heat and starts breaking down) so that the oil can get hot enough to cook food without burning. Hence this simple rule: The clearer an oil, the higher its smoke point and the more neutral its taste. The following are some common oils and how to wield them.

↓

PEANUT
Smoke point: 450°F/230°C
High smoke point plus subtle flavor equals deep-frying go-to.

CANOLA
Smoke point: 350° to 400°F/180° to 200°C
Crossbred *"Canadian oil, low acid"* is for everyday sautéing and searing or mixing with olive oil for a light vinaigrette.

GRAPESEED
Smoke point: 400°F/200°C and higher
Gets plenty hot for stir-fries and shallow pan-frying of fish and steaks. It's too pricey for a big deep-fry.

SUPERMARKET EXTRA-VIRGIN OLIVE
Smoke point: 375°F/190°C
Good for a quick sauté, which won't give it a chance to get super-hot.

UNFILTERED (I.E., FANCY) EXTRA-VIRGIN OLIVE
Smoke point: 320°F/160°C
Thick and cloudy with natural sediments; best for drizzling on finished dishes. Smokes too quickly for cooking.

Mushroom Pan Sauce for Steak

Making a sauce in the pan you just used to cook whatever the sauce will cover—in this case, a beautiful steak—is all about perception. It looks (and tastes) like it takes more time and training than it actually does. That's because the ingredients do a lot of the work for you—the meat, in a way, becomes part of the sauce. The fundamental technique here is called "deglazing," and it's one of those essential principles of cooking that chefs hesitate to give away because it's so easy. Truth is it's simple to master, and it will catapult your confidence as a cook in just a few minutes.

The first thing to understand is that it's a blessing to have little bits of meat stick to the pan when you're cooking proteins like beef, pork, or chicken because those bits become the foundation of the sauce. The technical term for these little caramelized jewels is "fond," and their flavor is everything here. Be careful not to burn them when you incorporate them into your sauce, because then the final product will taste . . . burned. So keep your heat moderate. Beyond that, it's hard to mess this up. And the real beauty of deglazing lies in its speedy efficiency. By the time your steak has rested after cooking, everything's ready to eat.

SERVES

1

(multiply for as many steaks as you are willing to make)

LEVEL *of* DIFFICULTY

WORTH THE EFFORT

REASONABLE

EASY

1 shallot
2 tbsp unsalted butter
½ cup/55 g brushed clean and sliced
    mushrooms*
About 6 tbsp/90 ml cabernet sauvignon
About 6 tbsp/90 ml beef or chicken stock
Coarse salt and freshly ground
    black pepper
Handful of chopped fresh herbs such
    as parsley, chives, or tarragon or
    a mixture

1. In a hot, heavy-bottomed skillet (preferably cast iron and what you just cooked your steak in) over medium heat, add the shallot and 1 tbsp of the butter. When the butter has melted, add the mushrooms. Sauté the mushrooms for a few minutes, then stir in the wine and deglaze the pan by using your spoon to scrape up any browned bits from the bottom of the pan.

2. Cook until the liquid is reduced by half. Add the same amount of stock and cook to reduce that by half, too. Add a pinch of salt, some grinds of pepper, and the herbs. Finish by swirling in the remaining 1 tbsp butter.

You can use button, shiitake, cremini, oyster, or pretty much whichever mushrooms look good at the supermarket.

Forget the Noise

TOM CHIARELLA

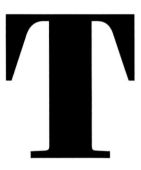

HE CHEF WANTS me to use one pan. One bowl. One spoon. He wants me to do my work in a single corner of one table in one of nine kitchens tucked into the labyrinth of tunnels beneath the new Horseshoe Casino in Cincinnati, three of which are devoted to the scale and service of the sprawling casino buffet, which serves German, Asian, Italian, American, and Mexican food, plus a separate salad bar, soup-and-bread station, and dessert spread. Ovens are wired to the chef's computer; walk-in freezers are matched by walk-in ovens. Pallets of mayonnaise sit on the polished concrete loading dock.

But the chef, Pete Ghione, asks that I ignore all that. I came here to learn what I could from a chef who cooks for thousands of people a day, and his first lesson is: Cooking is a small job. Finite work. One simple task connected to the next. Right now, he wants me to pick up a Roma tomato, core it, and cut it lengthwise. That is my job.

Casinos always toy with scale. I once stood in a tunnel beneath the Mirage Hotel in Las Vegas, where I got to shake hands with both Siegfried and Roy. Just as my brother and I were about to get our photo taken with them, the four of us were forced to make way for a kitchen worker pushing a spotless cart of beautifully chopped iceberg lettuce. Three cubic yards of it. Somehow astounding. We all stared silently at the scale of the thing. "Zhat is for buffet," Roy whispered to me, as if that explained things. Or excused them. His breath smelled like parsley.

When you're sitting at that blackjack table in the middle of four million square feet of slots and showgirls and hospitality suites, the whole universe is you and your three hundred bucks. Distance, size, and perspective are fun-house-mirrored. That may be why Ghione is teaching me three compact, quiet, reliable recipes in the middle of the hubbub. One corner of one counter. He describes each dish—orange-chicken tacos, avocado salad, charred tomato salsa—as a series of isolated yet interdependent steps. "You don't have to make things more complicated. You don't have to cook too much food or food that requires every bit of your energy. You just have to make good elemental food. You present it that way and it works on a kitchen table in an apartment or on a huge buffet line." There is no difference, he is saying, between us—me, a guy who cooks at home for a few people at a time, and him, with his clientele of hungry hordes.

Oil the grill, not the tomatoes. This keeps them from getting greasy and overmoist. Little lessons spill out of him. "Simplicity matters more to me because it gives me the time to enjoy what I do. So I cook more, I guess," he says. "But I cook better food." Still, at first the lesson plan he has devised for me doesn't sound like enough work. Not enough that I'll learn from it. The salsa is simply six piles of vegetables, roasted and puréed. But immediately, he starts breaking it into steps, and in each step lies wisdom. Grill the onions first, to flavor the grill. Roast the tomatoes with the skin to the heat— keeps them from steaming, getting mushy. Time the roasting of the other vegetables around the tomatoes' roasting. When the tomatoes have blackened on the skin side, flip them over until the open side starts to show some black. Ghione wants me to work quicker, to be more systematic in turning the vegetables toward the heat.

"Being fast doesn't have anything to do with being a chef. It has to do with the changes you're bringing about in the food," he says. "Uniformity keeps it simple. You don't want to be problem-solving when you cook. You want to make something reliable and good. You need to work fast to keep things even. Don't doze your way through a dish."

I admit to him that I don't ever eat roasted tomatoes—too soupy, too lacking in texture. "But the taste is remarkable," he says. "The charred skin is key. That's a flavor you want—and texture is eliminated, because we'll purée it in the end."

The other kitchens surge toward the lunch buffet. Questions fly at Ghione. He answers without looking up. He is focused on this spot, where he and I work. Work the avocado in the cup of its skin. Mash it in there. You won't have to fool around with another bowl. His buffet chef checks in just as we finish the salsa, which we've blended in a food processor. Ghione's mind is on what he's about to eat. The three of us eat it on chips while it's still hot, right out of the food processor. They are two men at the front end of a massive parade of food, pausing to marvel at what six vegetables, roasted and blended just so, have become.

"We should serve this," the buffet chef says, jabbing at the salsa with a chip in his fingers. "Jeez, that's good. We should serve it warm, like this." We've made only the one bowl, a small pleasure in a vast space. This can be done again and again. Ghione's salsa is a master class in creating flavor.

Charred Tomato Salsa

Oil the grill more than the vegetables. This keeps them from getting greasy and overmoist. Always grill the onions first because they will flavor the grill. Working fast is not about showing off. It's about keeping things even so that there are no surprises.

SERVES

4

LEVEL *of* **DIFFICULTY**

WORTH THE EFFORT

REASONABLE

EASY

Canola oil
Sea salt
10 ripe plum tomatoes, cut in half lengthwise
6 scallions, stem ends removed
1 white onion, cut into slices about ½ in/12 mm thick
2 poblano chiles
2 red jalapeño chiles
10 sprigs fresh cilantro
2 garlic cloves, thinly sliced
Juice of 2 limes
½ tsp ground cumin
Freshly ground black pepper

1. Build a hot fire in a charcoal grill or preheat a gas grill to high. Brush the grill rack with canola oil.
2. Very lightly oil and salt the vegetables and chiles and arrange them on the grill rack, placing the tomato halves skin-side down. Grill until each piece is caramelized and tender—the skin will pucker and slightly blacken. Transfer each piece to a platter as they are done. Peel the skin and remove the stems from the chiles once they have cooled to the touch. Place all of the charred vegetables in a blender or food processor. Process to a purée and transfer to a serving bowl.
3. Place the cilantro (reserve a sprig for garnish, if desired), garlic, lime juice, and cumin in the blender or food processor (no need to clean it) and purée. Add to the charred vegetable purée in the bowl and stir to mix well. Taste for salt and pepper, adjust the seasoning, garnish, and serve warm or at room temperature.

Artichoke and Parmesan Dip

Preparing the fresh artichokes for this dip requires a bit of extra work, but this is no ordinary game-day crudité. It has the texture of a classic dip, great flavor, and it's healthful. You'll need to remove the tough outer petals from each artichoke until it's about half its original size. Then you'll need some dexterity: Cut about ½ in/12 mm off the stem and about 1 in/2.5 cm from the top after that. Split it lengthwise and remove the silky thistle and remaining thorny leaves from the center. Give them a good rinse and get moving, because you're probably close to the coin toss at this point.

SERVES

10

LEVEL *of* **DIFFICULTY**

WORTH THE EFFORT

REASONABLE

EASY

¼ cup/60 ml olive oil

12 artichokes, trimmed and cleaned (see recipe introduction)

2 white or red onions, sliced

Coarse salt and freshly ground black pepper

2 cups/480 ml dry white wine

1 cup/240 ml water

¼ cup/60 ml crème fraîche

2 cups/230 g freshly grated Parmesan cheese

1. In a large saucepan, gently heat the olive oil over medium heat. Add the artichokes and onions to the pan and sauté until slightly softened, about 5 minutes. Add a bit of salt and pepper, then add the wine and water, bring to a simmer, and cook till tender, 30 to 45 minutes depending on your definition of "gently."

2. Remove from the heat and let cool, then transfer the artichokes and onions and the remaining cooking liquid to a food processor. Process until smooth. Fold in the crème fraîche and cheese. Season with salt and pepper and serve.

TIP

You can serve this dip with fresh veggies, but I prefer it with toasted croutons. And a beer.

Pickled Jalapeños

These are crunchy and have a lot more heat than the limp, squishy, jarred varieties found in the supermarket. Even better, you'll end up with a nice spicy vinegar that you can add to greens, gumbo, or game-day Bloody Marys.

SERVES

LEVEL *of* DIFFICULTY

8 to 10 fresh jalapeño chiles
5 cups/1.2 L distilled vinegar
1 cup/200 g sugar

1. A couple days before kickoff, throw the jalapeños into a cast-iron skillet over medium heat and cook until they start to blister, about 5 minutes.

2. Meanwhile, in a 3-qt/2.8-L saucepan, bring the vinegar and sugar to a boil, stirring to dissolve the sugar.

3. Place the chiles in a heatproof glass or ceramic bowl and pour the vinegar solution over them. Let cool completely, then refrigerate until game time.

4. The jalapeños can be stored in the refrigerator in a glass jar, tightly covered with a lid, for about 1 month.

Pimento Cheese

A staple of the Southern table and school lunch box, pimento cheese is more than a dip. It's a dip with backbone, better suited to the barstool than to a tea party. Sure, it works on crisp pieces of cold celery, toasted bread, Triscuits, and itty-bitty finger sandwiches. But you can spread it on a burger, make grilled cheese, or drip it into an omelet. You can eat it right out of the refrigerator. No one doesn't like it.

SERVES

8

LEVEL of DIFFICULTY

WORTH THE EFFORT

REASONABLE

EASY

Home-roasted peppers are best, but you can use good-quality jarred red peppers—preferably in olive oil, but peppers in a brine are okay, too.

Shredding is best done when the cheese is cold, but mixing works better when the cheese is at room temperature.

4 oz/115 g cream cheese, softened

¾ cup/170 g Duke's mayonnaise (Hellmann's, if you live up north)

¼ cup/30 g diced roasted red bell pepper*

½ tsp salt

½ tsp freshly ground black pepper

2 tsp hot sauce

2 lb/910 g shredded mixed good-quality white and orange extra-sharp Cheddar cheese**

1. In a bowl, break down the cream cheese with the back of a wooden spoon and combine with the mayonnaise, stirring well so there are no lumps. Add the bell pepper, salt, black pepper, and hot sauce and stir to combine.

2. Add the cheese in handfuls, using the wooden spoon or a wooden spatula to mash and stir. Once the cheese starts to blend and have some flow, start folding it over and under. You are not going for smooth here. The mixture should be thick and lumpy. Refrigerate for 30 minutes before serving.

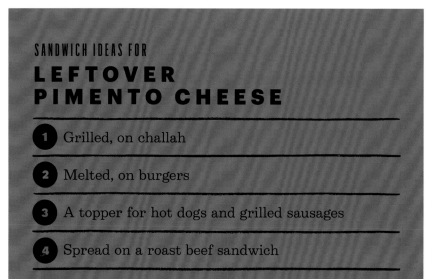

SANDWICH IDEAS FOR
LEFTOVER PIMENTO CHEESE

1 Grilled, on challah

2 Melted, on burgers

3 A topper for hot dogs and grilled sausages

4 Spread on a roast beef sandwich

STEPHEN STRYJEWSKI | COCHON | *New Orleans, Louisiana*

Fromage Fort

I don't see the far side of 1:00 A.M. as often as I used to, but in an earlier life I would cook late quite a bit. I liked steak seared in a cast-iron skillet with lots of whole butter and sea salt because of the ease of preparation and cleanup. Large portions of my life were fueled by ramen, and sandwiches rank high (the BLT, the Fluffernutter). And despite the carnauba-wax taste, I have an unnatural love for ice cream with Magic Shell.

When I'm feeling fancy, I make *fromage fort*, a classic French way to use up choice cheese scraps. To write a recipe almost seems crazy—you can use just about any cheese pieces you have (although I avoid blues, since they dominate). Firm cheeses like Cheddar in combination with triple crèmes like Camembert or Brie work well. It's a great thing to have on hand for late-night eating, whether you spread it on toasted bread, eat it with crackers, or use it as a topping for Tater Tots, which I call the Double Whammy (see below).

SERVES

12

(as a snack, or 8 for hungry snackers)

LEVEL of DIFFICULTY

WORTH THE EFFORT

REASONABLE

EASY

The more soft cheese you use, the less butter you add.

2 lb/910 g cheese ends and pieces, at room temperature
½ cup/120 ml dry white wine
4 to 5 tbsp/55 to 70 g unsalted butter at room temperature*
2 garlic cloves
Freshly ground black pepper
Toasted bread or crackers for serving

1. Remove and discard any hard rinds from the cheese. Place the cheese in a food processor. Add the wine, butter, and garlic and season with pepper; buzz until smooth, 2 to 3 minutes. Taste and add more pepper if needed. (Rarely does it need salt.) If you're saving some for another night, transfer to containers, cover, and refrigerate for a few days. **2.** Eat cold with bread or crackers or let warm up at room temperature to soften a bit.

EXTREMELY **EASY** RECIPE

DOUBLE WHAMMY

Place **TATER TOTS** in a pan and cook in a hot oven according to the package directions, adding a little **EXTRA OIL** and shaking the pan occasionally to get them browned and crisp. When the tots are done, spoon some *FROMAGE FORT* over the top and place under a hot broiler until it melts and bubbles, no longer than 2 minutes. Serves as many Tots (and *fromage*) as you got.

MICHAEL MINA | MICHAEL MINA | *San Francisco, California*

Bourbon Baked Beans

Take some beans, add some bourbon and some bacon, and you've got a recipe for magic.

SERVES

6

LEVEL of DIFFICULTY

WORTH THE EFFORT

REASONABLE

EASY

1 lb/455 g navy beans
8 oz/230 g bacon, chopped
1 yellow onion, minced
2 tbsp tomato paste
2 tbsp molasses
1 tsp dry mustard
½ cup/60 ml chili sauce
½ cup/60 ml bourbon
½ cup/60 ml strong coffee
1 cup/155 g very finely chopped
    (to a pulp) fresh pineapple
1 cup/200 g firmly packed
    brown sugar
Freshly ground black pepper
Pinch of red pepper flakes
Coarse salt

1. Soak the beans in enough water to cover double their volume overnight. In the morning, discard the water and rinse the beans.

2. In an 8-qt/7.5-L pot, cook the bacon over medium heat. Once the bacon has started to brown slightly, add the onion and sweat until translucent. Stir in the tomato paste and cook for 1 minute. Add the soaked beans, molasses, mustard, chili sauce, bourbon, coffee, pineapple, and brown sugar. Season with black pepper and red pepper flakes. (Don't add any salt yet; it will keep the beans from softening if added early.) Bring to a simmer, then turn the heat to low and cook for 4 to 6 hours, or until the beans are soft.

3. Once the beans have softened, season with salt and cook 1 hour more. You may have to add a little water to maintain the consistency. If the beans are still too wet after the allotted cooking time, then raise the heat to medium and simmer until the desired consistency has been reached.

FRANCINE MAROUKIAN | **THE WORKSHOP KITCHEN** | *Philadelphia, Pennsylvania*

Chicken Soup

One Thursday night a few years ago, in the comfort and security of my own pajamas, I saw my awful old boyfriend on *Seinfeld*. He was dating Elaine, and I watched the progress of their courtship with the foreboding of a film fanatic who recognizes every plot twist. "Don't do that, Elaine," I counseled from the couch.

What if my awful old boyfriend succeeded in wooing Elaine and became a regular thing on the one night I must see TV? I had only myself to blame. I had done more than school him in the ABCs of dating—I had passed on enough knowledge to please even the most extravagantly difficult woman: I had taught him to cook chicken soup.

Homemade chicken soup, the theory goes, has magical powers to heal everything from a cold to a bad case of the blues. Preparing it requires planning and waiting, teaching the cook to prolong and then fulfill desire, a compelling duality that became the foundation of my awful old boyfriend's now frequently televised charisma. I suspect it was our private lessons that turned him into a leading man, soup to nuts.

SERVES

8

LEVEL *of* **DIFFICULTY**

WORTH THE EFFORT

REASONABLE

EASY

---

3 qt/2.8 L chicken stock

2 qt/2 L water

4 whole bone-in, skin-on chicken breasts, split in half (8 pieces)

2 tbsp unsalted butter

2 tbsp olive oil

3 yellow onions, diced

10 stalks celery, diced

10 carrots, peeled and diced

Freshly ground black pepper

2 tbsp finely chopped fresh thyme

Kosher salt

2 bunches broccoli, trimmed to the bud clusters and separated into tiny florets

1. In a large stockpot (at least 6 qt/ 5.7 L) over medium-high heat, combine the stock, water, and chicken breasts and bring to a gentle boil. Lower the heat and simmer until the chicken is cooked though, about 25 minutes. Remove the chicken, let cool, and shred meat into bite-size pieces.
2. Strain the cooking liquid through cheesecloth (or a fine-mesh strainer) and reserve. Thoroughly wipe out the stockpot and return to medium heat.

Melt the butter in the olive oil until foaming, then add the onions, celery, and carrots and cook, stirring occasionally, until the vegetables begin to exude their moisture ("sweat"), 10 to 12 minutes. Stir in 2 tsp pepper and 1 tbsp of the thyme. Cook for several more minutes, stirring often, until the edges of the onions begin to color. Add the reserved cooking liquid and return to a boil. Lower the heat and simmer, uncovered, until the flavors marry and the vegetables are tender, about 35 minutes. Season with salt and add the remaining thyme and more pepper, if needed.
3. Just before serving, remove the pot from the heat. Add the shredded chicken and broccoli florets, letting the soup to sit long enough so the chicken is warmed through (without becoming rubbery) and the broccoli is crisp-tender and beautifully colored, 3 to 5 minutes.

The Kitchen Rules
(Abridged)

FRANK CASTRONOVO AND FRANK FALCINELLI, FRANKIES SPUNTINO

A FEW HELPFUL thoughts from two ascendant chefs. Antipasto is what you throw at the wolves before they eat so you're not stressed. Plus, when everyone has their own little appetizer plate at their place around the table—"this is mine, that's yours"—that's not Italian. That's why we like antipasti: Anything goes. You pile it on platters and set them out before a meal, and people grab what they want—using toothpicks, or small plates, whatever—and eat it. You have your basics—sliced cured meats, cheeses, roasted vegetables (see the technique opposite), olives. But to enhance an antipasto, you can add marinated mushrooms. You can put lentil salad, or bean salad. Little bit of this, little bit of that, it just keeps coming at you. Anchovies. If you cooked a big steak the night before, slice some and put it out.

NEVER USE A CHEAP OLIVE OIL

In cooking, you have proteins, carbs, and fats, and your fat should be the best quality you can get. Our food is sometimes only three or four ingredients—but if three ingredients are playing in a band and one guy isn't playing so good, it doesn't sound right. Any time you put quality olive oil on something, it's *sparkle sparkle sparkle*. If it's crap, then it's *crap crap crap*.

OWN THESE THREE ITEMS

Knife, bowl, pot. You need to cut, you need to mix, you need to cook.

COOK BETTER PASTA

Fresh pasta: It's done when it floats to the top, 2 or 3 minutes. Dry pasta: Taste it. Then taste it again a minute later. You shouldn't be walking away from the stove anyway. What do you need to do for 8 minutes that's so important? Stick around. Have a drink. Because the box isn't right. If the box says 7 minutes, start tasting after 4 minutes. When you bite it, look at the cross section so you can see how much the water has penetrated—you want just a tiny bit of white in the middle.

TASTE WHILE YOU COOK

Don't wait till the end. How do you know what you're doing? Taste and season every step of the way.

DON'T OIL THE PASTA WATER

Giving the pasta a good stir about 30 seconds after adding it to the pot will keep it from sticking together.

ON COOKING WITH OIL

There are better cooking oils than olive: sunflower, grapeseed, canola, in that order. They don't burn. Start it in the pan cold, bring up the heat slowly. If you want olive oil flavor, start with one of those, then add a little olive oil.

HOW TO ROAST VEGETABLES

Lightly coat them with olive oil so they'll caramelize without getting limp. Hit them with salt and pepper. Spread them on a baking sheet, not too crowded. Roast and serve at room temperature. Here's a chart to get you started.

ROAST	AT 350°F/180°C	READY WHEN
Brussels sprouts	25 minutes	Browned and crisp outside, tender when squeezed
Carrots	45 minutes	Offer no resistance to fork tines
Sweet potatoes	45 minutes	Offer no resistance to fork tines; should squish if squeezed
Cauliflower	45 to 50 minutes	Mottled and brown; should have a crisp-tender chew, like popcorn

THE MOST ESSENTIAL CHEESE

Parmigiano-Reggiano gets the glory, but pecorino romano costs about a third less and it's stronger in that earthy, grandma's-cooking flavor, so you need less of it. If you see Parmigiano in a recipe, you can use pecorino.

HOW TO BREAD ANYTHING

Three bowls: flour, egg wash (beaten eggs or whites), and bread crumbs. You take your meat or vegetable or whatever, you dredge it in the flour, dunk it in the egg wash, then coat it with bread crumbs. And fry it. If you want thicker crust, do it again—the double bread. You can flavor your flour, your egg wash, or your bread crumbs—cayenne, salt and pepper, whatever you want to put in there.

RELAX

Don't be afraid. Cook with love, or it won't come out well. Put your music on, get in the mood, have a drink. And then, one day, cooking just clicks, like when you figure out how to pedal a bike. You understand the one-two-threes, then you can improvise. And you discover that the trick to cooking the way we do is, there is no trick.

The Chef Comes to the Supermarket

An exploration of the A&P in Hoboken, New Jersey, after which you'll never walk through a grocery store the same way again.

TOM COLICCHIO

Tom Colicchio, who grew up not far from here, in Elizabeth, enters the A&P at midday. It is a cavernous and well-lit hangar. There's a cheese case not far from the front door. On a shelf above a pile of Camembert are jarred sweet Peppadew peppers, which are about the size and shape of hollowed-out golf balls.

See, what you could do is take some of these, get some canned tuna in olive oil, and stuff the peppers with tuna. Great little appetizer—just stuff 'em. If you bought the same thing at an Italian market in Manhattan, it would cost you twelve bucks for a jar of maybe six peppers.

You look around, you think of ways to use things. It's what we're taught in restaurants: Use everything.

The chef wanders down an aisle of jars and cans. A large middle-aged woman says to the even larger middle-aged woman sluggishly pushing a cart a few yards behind her, "Come on, Pookie." Colicchio notices this but focuses instead on a rack of marinated antipasto ingredients.

You could go get a can of cooked beets, some *giardiniera [a mix of pickled cauliflower, carrots, and peppers]*, a jar of artichokes, roasted peppers, oil, and vinegar, and you got a great salad.

Okay, here we go. *[He is now in the soup aisle. Colicchio has the same enthusiasm for the supermarket as a source of discovery that you imagine he would at the local farmers' market, or at a good fishmonger.]* A can of vegetable minestrone. Let's not look at this as a soup. Let's look at it as a bunch of vegetables in a sauce. Add it to pasta. Or better than that, say you have a lamb chop. You could drain this and use the vegetables as a garnish on the lamb chop. You haven't washed or chopped a thing. When I was at Mondrian *[a restaurant in midtown Manhattan where Colicchio earned a three-star review in 1990 and was named one of America's best new chefs]*, I did a rack of lamb with minestrone. Same thing, kind of.

Take split-pea soup. Buy a smoked ham hock and cook it in the split-pea soup. The ham hock is already cooked, so all you're doing is heating everything up, and you've re-created a classic dish.

If you want to feel like you're really cooking, buy a can of black bean soup and a jar of chile peppers. Steam some clams open in water and garlic—or white wine—and mix in the black bean soup and some of the chiles, and some cilantro. Whoa.

The A&P has a section of Asian foods that is as big as a small Asian market.

This is a great section. These are all just cooking sauces. Same idea as the cream of mushroom. Buy some shrimp, cook 'em, add 'em to the curry sauce, you're done. You could also use these sauces as a rub. Rub it on a piece of meat and grill it. That's instead of making your own rub of curry powder, turmeric, coriander seed, cardamom, garlic. . . .

I'm thinking I might come out from the city and shop at this store sometime.

Colicchio picks up a bag of chicharrones, which are fried pork rinds, and smiles.

Texture. You could put these on top of a stir-fry. Use them to crust chicken, the way people do with cornflakes. Crushed plantain chips would work, too.

He finds himself in the vast produce section, standing before what seems like seventy-five thousand apples.

My wife makes a crumble: fruit mixed with a tiny bit of flour, and then for the topping you just mix butter and instant oatmeal.

Over by the cheeses again, there's an odd case containing tubs of pickles, foil bags of brandade, packaged ravioli, and pierogies wrapped in plastic. The pierogies are attractive. There's a little label with the name of the bakery stuck on the plastic.

I went to a Ukrainian kindergarten. Twice a week, the lunch ladies would make pierogies and sell them to the public. Oh, they were so good. And see, these actually look good. They look like somebody, a person, actually *made* them. You know?

FRANCINE MAROUKIAN AND TONY AIAZZI | THE WORKSHOP KITCHEN | *Philadelphia, Pennsylvania*

Dark and Stormy Pineapple

The Dark and Stormy, a classic summer cocktail of ginger beer, rum, and lime, has a nineteenth-century nautical past linked to the rum runs between the United Kingdom and the Caribbean. This grilled dessert pays tribute.

SERVES

LEVEL *of* **DIFFICULTY**

WORTH THE EFFORT

REASONABLE

EASY

2 ripe pineapples
2 tbsp peeled and chopped fresh ginger
1 cup/200 g firmly packed dark
   brown sugar
½ tsp freshly ground black pepper
6 oz/90 ml dark rum
1 lime

1. Build a medium-hot fire in a charcoal grill or preheat a gas grill to medium.

2. Cut off the top and bottom of the pineapples so they sit flat. One at a time, sit a pineapple upright on its flat end and, using a sharp chef's knife, cut off the rind from top to bottom, following the contour of the fruit and on working your way around. Cut deep enough to get behind the "eyes" (brown spots) of the pineapples, about ¼ in/6 mm. Turn the peeled pineapples onto their sides and cut into slices about 1 in/2.5 cm thick.

3. In a bowl, mix together the ginger, brown sugar, pepper, and rum and smear over the pineapple slices.

Arrange on the grill rack and grill over low heat until nicely grill-marked and golden all over (watch carefully, as the sugar may burn quickly), turning when the edges start to caramelize. Move the slices around often to different heat areas to get even caramelizing. The timing is very subjective, probably around 15 minutes.

4. Transfer the pineapple to a platter, squeeze the lime's juice over, and serve immediately.

TIP

Serve either with something sweet, such as dulce de leche ice cream, or savory, such as grilled tuna or salmon.

Elote Salad

Elote **(or corn on the cob)** is a Mexican street food, eaten on a stick or by using the peeled-down husks and cob as a handle. Here, it's an outdoor salad—easier to prepare, serve, and eat.

SERVES

LEVEL *of* **DIFFICULTY**

WORTH THE EFFORT

REASONABLE

EASY

CHILE-LIME MAYO
1 cup/225 g mayonnaise
Juice of 1 lime
1 tsp mild chile powder
½ tsp smoked paprika
2 tsp hot sauce

12 ears corn, in husks
1 cup/60 g coarsely chopped fresh
    cilantro
6 scallions, sliced
1 cup/115 g Cotija cheese, crumbled
Mild chile powder for dusting

1. TO MAKE THE CHILE-LIME MAYO: In a bowl, stir together all the mayo ingredients until well mixed. Refrigerate for up to 3 days.

2. In a big pot or pail, soak the corn in its husks in cold water for at least 1 hour. Use a smaller lid or plate as a weight to keep the cobs submerged.

3. Build a medium-hot fire in a charcoal grill or preheat a gas grill to medium.

4. Arrange the corn in its husks around the outer edges of the grill, where the heat is low. (The steam from the soaking period will cook the corn.) As the corn cooks, using tongs, turn each cob a quarter turn every 5 minutes or so, to cook it evenly. When the husks are toasted all around, 20 to 25 minutes, transfer the corn to a platter and set aside to cool. When cool enough to handle, shuck the corn. Add a few coals to the grill to keep it at medium heat.

5. When the corn is shucked, return it to the grill and lightly char on all sides, turning as needed, about 10 minutes total. Do this dry—no oil or salt or pepper.

6. Cut the kernels from the corncobs. One at a time, stand each cob in the center of a large roasting pan (to catch the falling kernels). Slice down the ear with a knife and work your way around, cutting off the kernels as close to the cob as you can without digging into the cob. The knife must be flat. If it's angled and the blade digs into the cob, you won't have an easy time of it (like trying to mow the lawn with a hoe).

7. In a serving bowl, combine the grilled corn with the spicy mayo along with the cilantro and scallions, mixing well to coat. Mix in most of the cheese and scatter the rest over the top, along with a dusting of chile powder. Serve immediately.

The Pantry Hall of Fame

An enshrinement of the best heirloom kitchen-cupboard products, from a time when being a locavore meant foraging for ingredients in your own cabinets.

FRENCH'S FRENCH FRIED ONIONS
1950s (then known as Durkee Famous Foods)

It's hard to come up with another single ingredient so solely identified with one dish: these fried onions as the crunchy topping on the legendary creamy green-bean casserole invented by Dorcas B. Reilly, a kitchen supervisor for Campbell's Soup. The original recipe is in the National Inventors Hall of Fame.

LIPTON ONION SOUP MIX
1950s

Before chips came in assorted flavors, dips did the heavy lifting at parties, and the de rigueur cocktail combination—called "California dip" in honor of its home state—was sour cream and onion-soup mix: creamy salt meets crunchy salt. The dehydrated mix was also used as a "secret" ingredient in meat loaf or sprinkled directly on meat, like a spice rub.

SRIRACHA
Early 1980s

The newest home staple in the making, this spicy American-produced version of classic Asian chile sauce, in its clear plastic squirt bottle with bright-green top and rooster logo, has become ubiquitous—first in pho, noodle, and bánh mì shops and food trucks, then in the kitchens of star chefs, and now in the condiment aisle of your supermarket.

PUMATE SAN REMO SUN-DRIED TOMATOES
Early 1980s

They weren't always a culinary cliché. When first imported from the San Remo region of Italy by Giorgio DeLuca (for the original Dean & DeLuca, then the high cathedral of specialty food on Prince Street in SoHo), those meaty tomatoes, dried in the sun and packed in oil, tasted exotic and luxurious, like layering plump, saturated dollar bills into your sandwich.

RICE-A-RONI
Late 1950s

Vincent DeDomenico, a son of the Golden Grain Macaroni business in San Francisco's Mission District, came up with this early example of cross-cultural convenience food when he re-created an Armenian neighbor's rice pilaf by combining dry chicken-soup mix with bits of vermicelli and rice to produce the "San Francisco treat."

CAMPBELL'S CONDENSED CREAM SOUPS
Early to mid-1900s

Mushroom, chicken, and celery: What are these rich casserole thickeners but America's instantly convenient versions of French cuisine's white, creamy béchamel, one of its five revered classical mother sauces, making it possible for even novice home cooks to pour "fancy" right out of a can?

BETTY CROCKER CAKE MIXES
1940s

Although everything about its fictitious kitchen expert Betty Crocker was meant to be homey, "her" most famous product was the epitome of factory-food efficiency: a cake made from powder, in a box. At first, the mix required the addition of only water. But "industrial psychologists" on Madison Avenue in the 1950s determined that a housewife would buy more if she made a bigger contribution, to make her feel as though she were nurturing her family. Thus the mix was changed to require the addition of fresh eggs. Now that's *real* baking.

JELL-O
Late 1890s

JELL-O had its sensible, plain-Jane, school-lunch existence. But it also led a glamorous second life as a base for fanciful molds, magically suspending fruit and vegetables in ornately shaped and colorfully translucent gelatin, the glistening, quivering centerpiece on many a table set for "company."

KELLOGG'S CORN FLAKES
Late 1890s

The Kellogg brothers invented the first process for flaking corn at their Battle Creek Sanitarium, a health-conscious retreat for the wealthy. But as popular as corn flakes became as a cereal, their omnipresence made other uses inevitable, from a perfect crunchy coating for baked chicken and fish to the crumbled topping upon endless tuna noodle casseroles.

MARSHMALLOW FLUFF
1920s

There it was on the shelf in that big-bellied jar, just waiting to be finger-scooped: white and sticky and indestructible, like whipped Styrofoam. The more civilized made Fluffernutters or confections like Mamie's Million Dollar Fudge, a timeless recipe from the former First Lady that's now on file at the Dwight D. Eisenhower Presidential Library and Museum.

BISQUICK
1930s

Before we became a nation of gluten-free Spartans, moms used this revolutionary all-purpose mix ("A World of Baking in a Box") to whip up pancake pillows, which kids slathered in Log Cabin syrup. (Betty Crocker now makes rice-flour Bisquick in an earthier brown-toned box.)

KRAFT GRATED PARMESAN
1940s

Oh, for the simple days when we slid back the rotating, perforated yellow-disk cover and shook the shiny green cylinder until cheese rained down upon our spaghetti-and-meatball mountain, like perfect movie-set snow.

Asparagus and Morels (or Almost Any Vegetable, Really)

I'm a chef who grew up in the era just before the greenmarket revolution. Like so many others, my mother was a Birds Eye queen, and the Jolly Green Giant was her best friend, always hiding in the cupboard. So as I grew older and my passion for food grew, I wanted to come up with a simple, tasty, and healthy way to prepare garden or greenmarket vegetables. After many years of cooking, I find myself always returning to this one tried-and-true technique. It never fails me, and my guests always want to know how I did it. Simplicity, I tell them. The secret lies in the technique, and after a couple tries, you'll pick it right up. To use a restaurant phrase, it's done *à la minute*—"in a minute," or done to order. The goal is a reduced sauce clinging to vegetables that still have their picked-from-the-garden taste.

There's another phrase in professional kitchens: *mise en place*, meaning all the ingredients prepped and in place before you start cooking. So now when I tell you these vegetables go from *place* to plate in about 4 minutes, you know what I mean.

SERVES

(but easily repeated to serve more)

LEVEL *of* DIFFICULTY

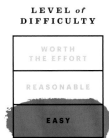

WORTH THE EFFORT

REASONABLE

EASY

1½ tbsp unsalted butter
1 shallot, diced
8 oz/230 g pencil-thin asparagus, tough woody ends trimmed or snapped off, cut into 1-in/2.5-cm pieces on the diagonal
5 morel mushrooms, *cleaned** and halved
Leaves from 3 sprigs fresh thyme
¼ cup/60 ml chicken stock
Wedge of lemon
Coarse salt and freshly ground black pepper

1. Heat a skillet over medium-high heat. Add about half of the butter, the shallot, asparagus, morels, and thyme, swirling the pan to disperse.

2. When the vegetables start to soften and release their liquid ("sweat"), but before they pick up any color, add the chicken stock. It will sizzle and quickly come to a boil. Add the remaining butter, and as it melts, toss to coat the vegetables with sauce. There shouldn't be a pool in the pan.

3. Squeeze in the lemon juice and taste, adjusting the seasoning with salt and pepper if needed. (It will depend on the saltiness of the stock you use, so taste before you commit.) Serve immediately.

If you can't find morels, use 3 oz/85 g of another seasonal wild mushroom, like chanterelles or porcini—or shaved truffles, if you want to splurge.

To clean morels, first shake in a paper bag to loosen any dirt that may be hiding in the mushrooms' many nooks, then dunk them in a bowl of water and swish them around to get rid of any remaining crud. Do this just before using, as morels don't like to be wet for long.

TIP

Other excellent vegetable combinations: Sugar snaps and shaved hakurei turnips, corn kernels and shiitake mushrooms, English peas and fava beans, snow peas and sunchokes, haricots verts and summer squash.

Taste.
Smell.
Listen.
React.

TOM JUNOD

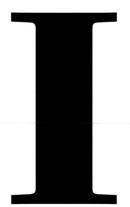

IDID EVERYTHING right. I cut up some bacon and put it in a pan. I removed the bacon when it was crisp, then put chopped onions in the fat. I added the lady peas and corn I had bought at a farm stand, then some cherry tomatoes, and got the whole thing bubbling. Some pasta, a dollop of fresh pesto—I expected my wife and daughter to greet it with applause, or at least the ravening hunger that is the home cook's true reward. I didn't get either. The dish was gray and soggy, stranded somewhere between a minestrone soup and a vegetable pasta. You couldn't taste the peas. My daughter provided the most damning criticism at a child's disposal: She asked for spaghetti with butter and cheese. It hit me that while I may be a pretty good home cook, I am not a home chef. I don't know how to "build flavors," as they say on the cooking shows. And so it was that two days after my pasta failure, I went to see Linton Hopkins.

Hopkins is the chef and owner of Atlanta's Restaurant Eugene. On the morning I drove to see him, I turned on the radio and there he was, talking not just about *Mastering the Art of French Cooking*, by Julia Child, but also about *The Iliad*, by Homer. He is

as stocky as a butcher and as bald as a monk, with a gap between his teeth and eyes that brighten like a baby's when he talks about food. When I arrived at his restaurant, he was standing in the kitchen, shaking a container of lady peas. There was a pale slab of smoked bacon on the steel counter, sweating in the warmth of the kitchen. With a small sharp knife, he cut off a piece and put it in a small pot, along with some water, some peas—he didn't measure—and some salt. Then he turned on the flame, bringing the peas to a boil, then down to a simmer. And then he kept on simmering them until he spooned a few out of the pot and squeezed one like a bug between his thumb and his forefinger. "You want to cook peas until you can smear them between your fingers. You added your tomatoes before you cooked the peas—well, the acid in the tomatoes stopped the peas from cooking. That's why you couldn't taste the peas."

He asked what I'd used for stock. I told him: a cardboard box. He said, "We all have to do that sometimes. But what a difference it will make if you make your own." He cut a couple chickens in half, old laying hens he'd gotten from his egg supplier that were stippled with yolk-yellow fat he didn't trim. "The fat is what gives the stock its taste and color," he said, and indeed, almost as soon as he put the hens in a pot with vegetables and water and set the pot to the flame, the yellow fat leached into the water and pooled atop its surface like beads of custard. "That's the color commercial-stock makers try to get by adding turmeric and other coloring agents."

Hopkins was not teaching me to cook, much less allowing me to cook. He was simply making lunch. But at every step of the way, he was showing me where I'd gone wrong—where I'd lost flavor and he built it. Flavor, he said, was not inherent in a recipe; it was inherent in the kitchen, in the accumulation of decisions made along the way, in the quality of the ingredients and the care you take with them. And that was the lesson: He was always cooking, he was never cooking. He hardly ever stirred; he tasted and smelled and listened. "Chefs stir because they want to feel like they're doing something. But I tell my chefs that observing is doing something. That's why I don't listen to music when I cook. You hear that?" he said, indicating the pan of onions sizzling with an insistent pneumatic hiss and caramelizing as thick as jam.

"That's my music. I hear that sound and I don't have to look at it. I know it's right."

And so: Don't break eggs against an edge but rather on a flat surface. Don't slice butter; shave it. Don't chop onions; section them. Add salt at every stage and you won't have to add so much at the end. When you add garlic to cooking onions, don't let it touch the pan; let the garlic steam atop the onions until you can smell it. Don't toast bread crumbs from the crust of the bread—it's already been toasted. And although "the world is a better place when you make your own mayonnaise," the mayonnaise is better "the farther away it is from a machine."

None of this seemed intimidating until I ate Hopkins's chicken fillets and perloo, which tasted not like the product of an accumulation of decisions but rather the most mysterious alchemy, all the flavor of the chicken fat finding its way into the unstirred rice that crusted at the bottom of the pan, all the smell of the pig smoke finding its way into the peas that sat for more than two hours in the water aggressively salted with mild Diamond Crystal. Lunch was so good it made me slightly dizzy when I ate it, and the next night, I tried applying what I'd learned to my pasta dish. I cooked the peas separately, with squiggles of supermarket bacon, and made my own stock with pale supermarket birds. I also banged around the kitchen for hours, filling the sink with a Thanksgiving's worth of pots and pans, and when I emerged from the tumult and served the dish to my family, two things were clear:

First, we could finally taste the peas.

And second, I was a beginner again.

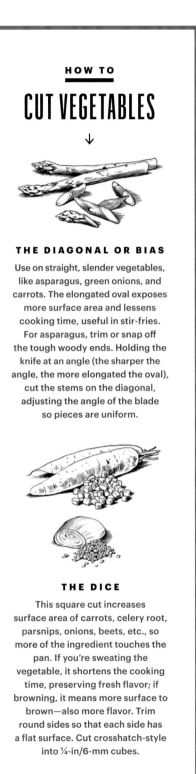

CUT VEGETABLES

↓

THE DIAGONAL OR BIAS

Use on straight, slender vegetables, like asparagus, green onions, and carrots. The elongated oval exposes more surface area and lessens cooking time, useful in stir-fries. For asparagus, trim or snap off the tough woody ends. Holding the knife at an angle (the sharper the angle, the more elongated the oval), cut the stems on the diagonal, adjusting the angle of the blade so pieces are uniform.

THE DICE

This square cut increases surface area of carrots, celery root, parsnips, onions, beets, etc., so more of the ingredient touches the pan. If you're sweating the vegetable, it shortens the cooking time, preserving fresh flavor; if browning, it means more surface to brown—also more flavor. Trim round sides so that each side has a flat surface. Cut crosshatch-style into ¼-in/6-mm cubes.

Perloo

You want to cook peas until you can smear them between your fingers. If you add the tomatoes before you cook the peas, well, the acid in the tomatoes stops the peas from cooking.

SERVES

6

LEVEL *of* DIFFICULTY

WORTH THE EFFORT

REASONABLE

EASY

2 cups/455 g lady peas, rinsed
One 2-in-/5-cm-square piece smoked slab bacon
1 qt/960 ml water
Kosher salt
¼ cup/55 g duck fat or chicken fat*
1 Vidalia onion, diced
½ green bell pepper, seeded and diced
1 stalk celery, diced
1 fresh bay leaf
3 tbsp minced garlic
5 whole canned San Marzano tomatoes, crushed by hand
2 cups/430 g Carolina gold rice
1 qt/960 ml chicken stock
¼ cup/15 g chopped fresh flat-leaf parsley
Freshly ground black pepper

1. Combine the peas, bacon, water, and 2 tbsp salt in a saucepan and bring to a boil. Lower to a simmer and cook until the peas are soft but still intact, 15 to 20 minutes. Remove from the heat and set aside.

2. In a large sauté pan with high sides and a lid, melt the duck fat over low heat, then add the onion, stirring to coat. Cook until very soft, 10 to 15 minutes. Add the bell pepper, celery, and bay leaf and cook until the vegetables are well softened. Spread the vegetable mix uniformly across the base of the pan and sprinkle the garlic over the top, letting the heat rising through the vegetables melt the garlic.

3. Add the tomatoes, raise the heat gently, and stir until the steam rises. (You don't want the vegetables browned, just lightly colored.) Add the rice, stir to coat, and add the stock, making sure the rice is well coated with the liquid. Bring to a simmer, add 1 tsp salt, and taste the broth; adjust with more salt until the broth tastes rich.

4. Drain the peas and add to the simmering liquid in a uniform layer, cover, and cook at a steady, low simmer until the rice is done, about 15 minutes. Remove from the heat, spread the parsley across the top, and let the dish sit for another 10 minutes for the rice to soften more and to allow the flavors to come together. Grind some black pepper on top and serve immediately.

Duck and chicken fat are available at butcher shops, good grocery stores, and from dartagnan.com.

Cooking for the Future

CHICKEN AND STEAK FOR SANDWICHES AND SALADS

With a minimum investment of kitchen time,
you can fill your fridge with enough sandwich and salad
basics to feed a weekend's worth of houseguests.

SKILLET-SEARED STEAK

With its bigger beefy taste and extra marbling that keeps the meat from drying out when refrigerated, economical boneless short ribs are a perfect cut for sandwiches. Other sandwich-worthy secondary cuts are sirloin flap and boneless chuck tenders.

Canola oil
3 boneless short ribs, about 1½ lb/680 g total, seasoned with a rub of your choice (a lemon pepper blend works great against the richness of the beef)

1. Preheat the oven to 375°F/190°C.
2. Lightly coat a cast-iron skillet with oil and heat until almost smoking. Sear the meat on both sides, about 5 minutes total, then transfer the skillet to the oven to finish cooking, about 15 minutes for medium-rare.
3. Transfer to a carving board and let the meat cool completely before wrapping and refrigerating (unsliced). When ready to use, carve the meat across the grain on the diagonal while it is still cold, then bring to room temperature.

SANDWICH IDEAS FOR LEFTOVER STEAK

1 With bread and butter pickles on a toasted English muffin

2 With pepper Jack cheese and salsa in a tortilla

3 With sliced cucumber, red onions, and watercress on crusty bread

4 Sliced, with melted Parmesan on garlic bread

POACHED CHICKEN BREASTS

The best way to keep chicken moist and tender for sandwich and salad usage is to poach the breasts, a short process you can pull off while working on other kitchen tasks.

2 large bone-in, skin-on chicken breasts, 12 oz/340 g each, split (or 4 bone-in, skin-on breast halves)
Big pinch of coarse salt
1 tsp black peppercorns
2 bay leaves

1. Rinse the breasts on both sides under cool running water. Place in a large pot; add water to cover; and add the salt, peppercorns, and bay leaves. Bring to a boil over medium heat, which should take at least 10 minutes. Rather than using intense heat, which can toughen chicken, you want to bring the heat up slowly so the breasts cook evenly and the meat stays silky tender.

2. As soon as the surface breaks into a boil, lower the heat and simmer the chicken breasts for 5 minutes. Remove from the heat and keep the breasts in the pot until the water cools, which will finish the cooking process.

3. Store with the skin and bone still attached so the chicken stays moist and keeps its shape. When ready to use, pull meat from bone and slice on the diagonal for sandwiches or into chunks for salad.

SANDWICH IDEAS FOR LEFTOVER POACHED CHICKEN

1 Sliced thinly, layered with ham, cheese, and honey mustard on a baguette with cornichons

2 Sliced thinly, layered with avocado and BBQ potato chips on a potato roll

3 Diced large, tossed with Greek salad

4 Diced large, tossed with sesame noodles

Black Pepper Beef Jerky

Drying as a means of preserving food has been around since before the pharaohs, and Native Americans used a combination of sun and wind to dehydrate their hunting bounty in anticipation of winter. The result was jerky (from the Spanish *charqui* meaning "dried meat"), a hardcore survival provision that was light enough to carry on the trail and could be eaten without telltale signs of a campfire, vital when traveling through dangerous territory. As the frontier colonized, settlers added cures and spice rubs that reflected their individual ethnic culinary traditions, creating an infinite variety of homespun recipes. Today, jerky still delivers a concentrated protein power that makes energy bars taste like nothing but candy.

SERVES

6

LEVEL *of* DIFFICULTY

WORTH THE EFFORT

REASONABLE

EASY

Liquid Smoke is strong stuff, made from smoking wet chips and then distilling that smoke into a liquid.

MARINADE
½ cup/120 ml molasses
½ cup/120 ml maple syrup (the real kind)
1 ½ cups/360 ml soy sauce
1 tbsp Liquid Smoke*
¼ cup/60 ml Worcestershire sauce
2 tbsp finely ground black pepper
1 tbsp garlic powder
1 tbsp onion powder

3 flank steaks, about 2 lb/910 g each
Canola oil

1. TO MAKE THE MARINADE: In a bowl, whisk together all of the marinade ingredients, making sure the molasses and maple syrup are fully dissolved and don't just sink to the bottom.
2. Holding the blade of a sharp chef's knife at a 45-degree angle and slicing diagonally, cut the steak across the grain into thin slices (no thicker than ¼ in/6 mm). →

The flank steaks will be easier to slice if you pop them in the freezer for an hour or two. Or you can ask your butcher to slice the meat for you.

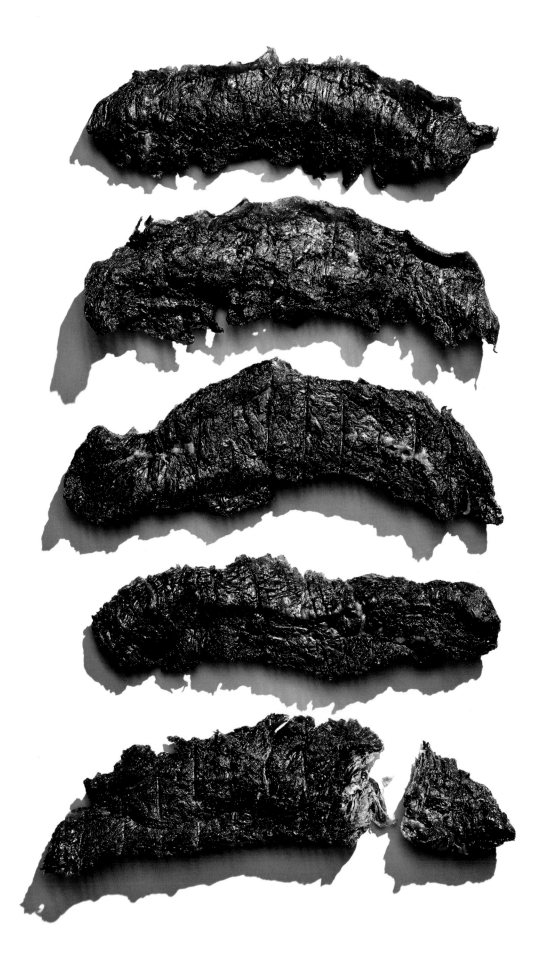

3. Whisk the marinade again and pour about one-fourth of it into a square-sided container, such as a glass baking dish. (The square shape is a better fit for the strips, making it easier to layer and keep the meat evenly covered.) Layer in the meat evenly, pouring more marinade over as needed to coat all pieces equally, pushing down each layer snugly.

4. Cover with plastic wrap, pressing the wrap directly to the top of the meat, and refrigerate for 24 hours.

5. The next day, dry the meat by layering the slices between paper towels to remove excess marinade (it will take several layers of towels). If the strips are too wet on the outside, they won't dry evenly in the oven and the excess liquid will drip down onto the oven floor.

6. Turn the oven to the lowest setting. Lay the meat out onto lightly oiled baking sheets, leaving a little space between each piece. Place a few sheets of aluminum foil on the bottom of the oven to catch drips and position the baking sheets directly on the oven racks, with nothing to block the air and heat from circulating around the oven. Leave the oven door cracked open throughout the drying process, which will take anywhere from 6 to 8 hours. Every 2 hours, flip the slices of meat and rotate the racks from top to bottom. (When flipping the jerky strips, move the drier ones to the front of the rack. It is always hotter in the back of the oven).

7. When the jerky is done, the strips should bend but not break. Let the jerky rest at room temperature for 1 to 2 hours after it comes out of the oven. This gives any moisture left inside the meat a chance to equalize with the drier outside surface. Store in an airtight container like a resealable bag or plastic container at room temperature for up to 3 months.

DO A BUNCH OF THINGS (A LITTLE) BETTER

↓

HOLD A KNIFE

Pinch the dull side of the blade with your pointer finger and thumb where the blade meets the handle. Wrap your other three fingers around the handle, leaving your thumb and pointer finger gripping the heel of the blade. Practice on a big bag of vegetables.

KELSEY NIXON,
host of **Kelsey's Essentials**

SCRAMBLE EGGS

For 2 eggs, add 2 tbsp water and 2 tbsp heavy cream, season with salt and freshly cracked black pepper, and whip the hell out of them with a whisk until frothy. Melt some butter over medium heat and cook the eggs, not touching them until they are partially set. Then start some light stirring until they're almost finished, and turn the heat off. They will finish cooking because the pan is still hot.

RANDY ZWEIBAN,
chef-owner, Province, Chicago, Illinois

MAKE A SANDWICH

Less is more. Proportion is key, making sure each element balances the next. I like a fresh slaw tossed in a light vinegar for some crunch and some acidity. Throw in the protein of your choosing, bearing in mind the salt that comes with cured or smoked meat. And when is adding a fried egg a bad thing? Butter the outside of your bread, griddle it, and that's a sandwich.

MICHAEL SCHWARTZ,
chef-owner, Michael's Genuine Food & Drink, Miami, Florida

COOK A LOBSTER

Use water that's as close to seawater as it can be—extremely salty or, better yet, seawater itself. And don't use much: Put 3 to 4 in/7.5 to 10 cm in the pot and, when the water is steaming like mad, add the lobster. A 1¼-lb/570-g lobster takes about nine minutes. Afterward, don't shock it in ice water. That makes the meat tougher. Just let it cool down.

DAVE PASTERNACK,
chef-owner, Esca,
New York, New York

MAKE A SPICE RUB

Start with spices that are whole (as opposed to ground) and fresh (as opposed to sitting in your cabinet for three years). Black pepper always goes well with coriander and mustard seed. Cinnamon always goes well with clove, anise, and allspice. Cardamom is usually too strong. Toast spices in a dry pan on the stove over low heat for a couple minutes, then grind them. (You can use a clean coffee grinder.) Then rub it on whatever meat you're cooking.

DAVID KATZ,
chef-owner, Mémé,
Philadelphia, Pennsylvania

SAUTÉ GARLIC

Start with a cold pan, add olive oil, then garlic, and turn burner to low heat. Through the gradual increase of temperature, you'll infuse the oil with the flavor of garlic while it turns slightly brown.

MARCO CANORA,
chef-owner, Hearth, New York, New York

BREAD MEAT

After you've breaded a piece of meat for pan-frying (dip in flour, dip in a water-and-egg-white mixture, dip in bread crumbs), spritz the breaded meat with a little water from a spray bottle. The moisture will prevent the crumbs from absorbing too much oil while still preserving that crispy crunch.

DAVID BURKE,
chef-owner,
David Burke Kitchen,
New York, New York

SEASON MEAT

Salt draws moisture out, so season just before sautéing meat or fish. If you salt too early, the surface of the flesh will become wet and will not get that nice golden crust. And if you marinate meat, remember to pat dry and season it just before you sear.

FRANK STITT,
chef-owner,
Highlands Bar and Grill,
Birmingham, Alabama

COOK CORN

Instead of boiling corn on the cob, dot it with a little butter, salt, and black pepper. Place on a baking sheet and roast in a 350°F/180°C oven until tender. Caramelize a little honey in a sauté pan and, when the corn comes out, brush with the honey.

ALEX GUARNASCHELLI,
chef-owner, Butter, New York, New York, and host of Alex's Day Off

GRILL FRUIT

Start with ripe, juicy fruit with a high moisture content. Lightly brush on all sides with melted butter or coconut milk. Make a dessert rub by combining 1 cup/200 g sugar with 1 tbsp cinnamon. Set up your grill for direct grilling—a preheated grate over a hot fire: Brush the grate clean with a stiff wire brush. Oil it with a paper towel folded into a tight pad, dipped in oil, and drawn across the bars of the grate. Oiling prevents sticking and gives you killer grill marks. Dip fruit in the rub to coat on all sides, shaking off excess. Grill the fruit long enough to turn the sugar and fruit juices into bubbling, golden caramel.

STEVEN RAICHLEN, *author of* The Barbecue Bible *and host of* Primal Grill

JUSTIN DEVILLIER | **LA PETITE GROCERY** | *New Orleans, Louisiana*

Spiced Apple Pie with Dulce de Leche

Growing up, there were always two sure signs that company was coming over: freshly washed fruit draining in a colander and a pie shell chilling in the fridge. It was a mysterious process. Either my mother or aunt would be the baker, and there was never much shared about the recipes. As I got older and became interested in baking, I studied and then practiced at family get-togethers—opening my skills to criticism improved my techniques quickly. I've always made my crusts from scratch, but even the ladies of the family use store-bought dough from time to time—and to be honest, you would never know the difference. The keys to perfecting your pie are to make a tasty, quality filling and pay close attention to cooking times.

Condensed milk, that gooey, sweet, canned cream featured in many classic American recipes, was another staple of our pantry. Like a lot of other products of its generation, condensed milk is all about preservation and shelf life. Canning was the idea of an early-nineteenth-century French confectioner who was looking for a way to preserve mass amounts of field rations for Napoleon's army. As America grew and families left the Atlantic seaboard to head west, they also left the open-air markets and grocers of their former cities. Without convenient access to daily provisions, the ability to preserve food became a matter of survival. Here, I use the condensed milk to cook a rich caramel sauce right in the can, intensifying its sweetness and creating a rich tan color. It's hard to think of anything more American than apple pie, and it seems only fitting to pair it with a pantry classic.

SERVES

8

(makes one 9-in/23-cm pie)

LEVEL of DIFFICULTY

WORTH THE EFFORT

REASONABLE

EASY

Two 14-oz/400-g cans Eagle Brand Condensed Milk, labels removed
5 Granny Smith apples, peeled, cored, and sliced
1 tbsp bourbon
1 cup/200 g granulated sugar, plus 2 tsp
1 tsp ground cinnamon*
¼ tsp freshly grated nutmeg
1 box Pillsbury prerolled piecrusts**
1 egg white, beaten
1 tsp coarse salt →

✳
If you have a whole stick of cinnamon and a rasp, grate the cinnamon instead of using ground cinnamon. Nutmeg too—it's often available whole, with a mini grater right in the jar.

✳✳
You'll find prerolled pie dough in the refrigerator case at the supermarket.

1. With a can opener, pierce two holes opposite each other in the tops of the cans of condensed milk. Place the cans in a medium saucepan, add water to reach up to 1 in/2.5 cm from the tops of the cans, and bring to a boil. Once boiling, turn the heat to medium-low to maintain a steady simmer (see Tip).

2. After 3 hours, remove the pot from the stove and let the cans cool in the hot water, about another 3 hours.

3. Meanwhile, preheat the oven to 350°F/180°C.

4. Place the apples in a large bowl. Add the bourbon, 1 cup/200 g sugar, cinnamon, and nutmeg and toss to coat.

5. Remove the piecrusts from the box and let stand according to the package directions. Roll one crust out to fit a 9-in/23-cm pie pan, the other slightly larger for the top. Fit the first piecrust into the pie pan and fill with the apples, mounding them slightly in the center. Top with the second crust. Crimp the edges to seal. With a small, sharp paring knife, cut an X in the center of the top crust to release steam during cooking. Brush with the beaten egg white and sprinkle with the 2 tsp sugar and the salt.

6. Place the pie on a baking sheet in the oven and bake for 45 minutes, then bump up the heat to 375°F/190°C. Bake until the pie is golden brown and bubbling, about 20 minutes more. Transfer to a wire rack and let cool, about 45 minutes.

7. Remove the milk cans from the water bath and open in the regular fashion. By this time, the resulting dulce de leche will have cooled, so you may want to reheat it slightly before serving: Warm it over low heat in a small saucepan filled with water that reaches halfway up the outsides of the can.

8. Cut the pie into wedges while still slightly warm. Serve with the warm dulce de leche spooned over the top.

TIP

IMPORTANT: *The level of the water should remain the same throughout the entire cooking process because the cans may explode if they are not nearly submerged. As you notice the water level going down, refill the pan.*

Men Don't Bake

TOM JUNOD

BAKING IS ABOUT everything that cooking is not—quantifying, keeping clean, preening, staying pure. But what the hell.

Most people are hungry, therefore they eat. I am hungry, therefore I cook. Since my senior year in college, when I moved into an apartment with a bunch of friends, I have cooked almost every day of my life. Cooking is, to me, the perfect fusion of generosity and selfishness, indeed the resolution of generosity and selfishness, the answer to my torn nature. I don't love to cook—I cook. It's what I do, and by this time, it's who I am.

There is something, however, I have never done as a cook. I have never baked. I have cooked thousands of meals big and small, but I have never cooked a cookie. I have never roasted a cake, or a pie. I have absented myself from the pleasures of baking bread, perhaps because baking bread is always presented in terms of pleasure—because people who bake bread never fail to get all poetic about its satisfactions ("the smell of baking bread in the morning"), and I don't want that kind of pressure. You don't need a cookbook to cook, but you can't bake without one, so there's something sort of sex-manual-y about baking, a doggedness to the rapture that is unhappily reminiscent of the '70s and trying to have sex to a Joni Mitchell album. I mean, sometimes you just want to *do it*, but you can't *just* bake a cake. You have to measure. You have to take as much time as it takes, with no shortcuts. You don't have to love cooking to cook, but you have to do more than love baking to bake. You have to bake out of love.

Which is why I found myself in the pastry kitchen of a New York restaurant that turns out something like four hundred desserts—four hundred expressions of love and pure-heartedness—a day. You see, my daughter loves cookies. I love my daughter. And yet I have never so much as sliced through a sludgy and eternal bar of premade dough so that she could have the experience of eating chocolate chip cookies "fresh out of the oven." I'm fine with Chips Ahoy!, as long as they come with a glass of milk. Still, I knew that eating homemade chocolate chip cookies would make my daughter happy, and so I visited the eminent pastry chef at Gramercy Tavern to find out not only how to make them but also why I was averse to making them.

I got my answer right away. "There are two kinds of people," Nancy Olson told me as soon as I showed up in her kitchen. "There are cooks, and there are bakers." Upstairs, there were cooks barking orders around rings of open flame that might have caused Vulcan to break a sweat; downstairs in Nancy's kitchen, there was just cozy warmth and flour-perfumed bakers working in silent accord. The cooks, of course, had something in common. So did the bakers. Indeed, when Nancy told me that everybody was either a cook or a baker, she might as well have said that everybody was either a man or a woman. You can cook like a man. But you can't bake like a man, because men don't bake. Nancy said that because baking is easy, it's hard; that because anyone can, a lot of men can't, or won't. "Theoretically anybody with a recipe should be able to do it. . . . You have to enjoy following instructions. You have to enjoy precision."

If cooking represents control, baking represents surrender. I wasn't going to learn how to make chocolate chip cookies from Nancy; I was going to learn how to *follow* the recipe to make chocolate chip cookies. In fact, no one knows how to make chocolate chip cookies, not even Nancy, who found a big binder with her recipe for Gramercy Tavern Chocolate Chip Cookies, opened it on one of her immaculate stainless-steel prep areas, and studied it like a monk with an illuminated manuscript. And that was the main difference between cooking and baking, it seemed to me: Humans have always known how to cook and have been able to pass their knowledge along, but nobody really knows how to bake, and so baking didn't exist until knowledge could be codified and written down—it didn't exist until the dawn of civilization. And that's what made me wary of it. I never want to feel particularly civilized when I cook, any more than I want to feel civilized when I write; indeed, refinement is the enemy of both.

And yet I baked with Nancy Olson. And I learned a few things about baking: Baking soda is what flattens cookies out, and so Nancy, who likes cookies to have "that nice domed shape," goes easy on it. Egg yolks are what give cookies that "fatty goodness, that rich gooeyness inside," and so she adds extra. And when breaking a lot of eggs, even professional bakers get bits of eggshell in the mixing bowl. But here's what they do to get them out: "Dip the large shell in the bowl. For some reason eggshells attract eggshells, and you can scoop them right out."

But I couldn't actually do anything with my newfound knowledge when I got home until Nancy sent me the recipe. I was something I haven't been in a kitchen in a long time—freaking helpless—and my helplessness continued even when Nancy started sending me encouraging e-mails and asking if I was having fun yet. Because I wasn't having fun. I was worried that I was making mistakes; and when my daughter pitched in, I started worrying that she was making mistakes. She's eight and makes eggs most every morning according to her own whims, dressing them with Japanese rice seasoning and soy sauce. But now when she asked, "Hey, Dad, what would happen if I squeezed some lemon juice in the batter?" I heard myself uttering the soul-crushing reply: "You'd ruin it."

The cookies were what Nancy wanted them to be, dome-shaped, crispy on the outside, moist on the inside, dense without being cakey, and revelatory of new textures with each bite. My daughter and I had succeeded in making the best chocolate chip cookies either of us had ever eaten, and I think what we were supposed to feel—the feeling that bakers are entitled to feel—was pride. But I hadn't cooked the cookies like a baker or baked the cookies like a cook; no, I had made the cookies like a father, and so what I felt were a father's emotions, sadness and relief, because I realized that I would never make them again.

NANCY OLSON | **FORMER PASTRY CHEF, GRAMERCY TAVERN** | *New York, New York*

Gramercy Tavern Chocolate Chip Cookies

All you have to do is follow the instructions. If you don't, it won't work. No pressure.

SERVES

6

(makes 14 large cookies)

LEVEL *of* DIFFICULTY

WORTH THE EFFORT

REASONABLE

EASY

10 tbsp/145 g unsalted butter, softened

1 cup plus 2 tbsp/225 g packed light brown sugar

1 large egg, plus 1 egg yolk

1½ tsp vanilla extract

1¾ cup plus 1 tbsp/170 g all-purpose flour

¾ tsp salt

½ tsp baking powder

⅛ tsp baking soda

1⅓ cups/250 g chocolate chips

1 cup/100 g walnuts, chopped

1. In the bowl of an electric mixer on medium speed, cream the butter and brown sugar until just thoroughly combined. (When done mixing, use a rubber spatula to scrape down to the bottom of the bowl; sometimes the paddle can't reach all the way down, leaving some of the mixture unmixed, so you have to do it by hand.)

2. With the mixer running, add the egg and egg yolk, one at a time, mixing the first one in before mixing in the second, then add the vanilla.

3. In a separate bowl, whisk together the flour, salt, baking powder, and baking soda.

4. Add the dry ingredients to the creamed ingredients, mixing just until almost completely combined.

5. Add the chocolate chips and walnuts and mix until just combined.

6. Cover and refrigerate for 30 minutes, or overnight.

7. Preheat the oven to 375°F/190°C. Using two soupspoons, divide the dough into 14 equal-size mounds. Place the mounds on two baking sheets, leaving about 1 in/2.5 cm between each cookie.

8. Bake for 14 to 18 minutes, or until the cookies are golden brown around the edges and set in the middle. Let cool on the baking sheet until fully set. Eat warm, of course.

Refrigerating the dough overnight is optional but makes for more uniformly baked cookies. The dough may also be rolled into a log and put in a resealable plastic bag, then stored in the freezer for up to 2 weeks. Slice off ½-in/12-mm cookies to bake. Cookies can be baked directly from the refrigerator or freezer.

Index

Credits

CHEF AND RECIPE CONTRIBUTORS:

Adam Sobel
Akhtar Nawab
Anthony Chittum
Bill Taibe
Brian Bistrong
Bryan Caswell
Bryan Voltaggio
Charlie Palmer
Chris DiMinno
Chris Jones
Christopher Kostow
David Myers
Donald Link
Edward Lee

Evan Mallett
Francine Maroukian
Frank Castronovo
Frank Falcinelli
Harold Dieterle
Jackie Shen
Jasper White
Jeff McInnis
Jeremy Sewall
John Fitzsimons
Jonathan Benno
Justin Devillier
Kevin Callaghan
Kevin Davis
Laurent Manrique
Lee Bailey

Linton Hopkins
Lydia Shire
Mario Batali
Matt Steigerwald
Mehdi Brunet-Benkritly
Michael Leviton
Michael Kaphan
Michael Mina
Michael Schlow
Michael Symon
Michael Toscano
Michael White
Mike Lata
Mitchell Rosenthal
Nancy Olson
Nemo Bolin

Nick Anderer
Pete Ghione
Ryan Poli
Roberto Donna
Seamus Mullen
Shane Solomon
Spike Gjerde
Stephen Stryjewski
Steven Satterfield
Ted Allen
Thomas Keller
Tom Colicchio
Tom Douglas
Tony Aiazzi
Tyler Cabot
Wolfgang Puck

RECIPE PHOTOGRAPHY CREDITS:

Page 15 (Adam Vorhees); pages 18 and 19 (Brad DeCecco); page 21 (Kenji Toma); page 24 (Ben Goldstein, Studio D); page 27 (Kenji Toma); page 29 (Philip Friedman, Studio D); page 32 (Grant Cornett); page 40 (Philip Friedman, Studio D); page 43 (Ben Goldstein, Studio D); page 49 (Jon Paterson, Studio D); page 53 (Philip Friedman, Studio D); page 57 (Marcus Nilsson); page 62 (Chris Eckert, Studio D); page 62 (Devon Jarvis); page 65 (Stacy Zarin-Goldberg); page 69 (Melissa Golden); page 71 (Jeffrey Westbrook, Studio D); page 74 (Ben Goldstein, Studio D); page 77 (Adam Levey); page 89 (Adam Vorhees); page 93 (Christopher Testani); page 101 (Grant Cornett); page 103 (Chris Collins) page 109 (F. Martin Ramin, Studio D); page 113 (J Muckle, Studio D); page 125 (Adam Vorhees); page 129 (Marcus Nilsson); page 135 (Joe DeLeo); page 138 (Philip Friedman, Studio D); page 141 (Ben Goldstein, Studio D); page 147 (Grant Cornett); page 149 (Adam Vorhees); page 159 (Grant Cornett); page 163 (Grant Cornett); page 165 (Marcus Nilsson); page 167 (Devon Jarvis, Studio D); page 173 (Deb Wenof); page 177 (Ben Goldstein, Studio D); page 181 (David La Spina); page 185 (J Muckle, Studio D); page 187 (Grant Cornett); page 195 (Ben Goldstein, Studio D); page 197 (Ben Goldstein, Studio D); page 200 (Aaron Graubart, Studio D); page 205 (Gregory Miller); page 209 (Will Styer); page 213 (Grant Cornett)

TRADEMARKS:

A&P grocery store is a registered trademark of The Great Atlantic & Pacific Tea Company; Abita is a registered trademark of Abita Brewing Company, LLC.; Ak-Mak is a registered trademark of Soojian's Inc.; Betty Crocker is a registered trademark of General Mills Inc.; Birds Eye is a registered trademark of Pinnacle Foods Group LLC; Bisquick is a registered trademark of General Mills Inc.; Campbell's is a registered trademark of CSC Brand LP; Chips Ahoy! is a registered trademark of Mondelēz International group; Cointreau is a registered trademark of Cointreau Société par actions simplifiée; Coleman is a registered trademark of The Coleman Company, Inc.; Crisco is a registered trademark of the J.M. Smucker Co.; Crock-Pot is a registered trademark of Rival Industries; Crystal Hot Sauce is a registered trademark of Baumer Foods, Inc.; Diamond Crystal is a registered trademark of Cargill Salt Company; Doritos is a registered trademark of Frito Lay, Inc.; DUKE'S is a registered trademark of The C.F. Sauer Company; Eagle Brand Condensed Milk is a registered trademark of the J.M. Smucker Company; Eggo Waffles is a registered trademark of the Kellogg Company; Food Network is a registered trademark of Television Food Network, G.P.; French's French Fried Onions is a registered trademark of Reckitt Benckiser Inc.; Gatorade is a registered trademark of the Gatorade Company; Gold's is a registered trademark of Gold Pure Food Products Co., Inc.; Gordy's is a registered trademark of Gordy's Pickle Jar, LLC; Gosling's is a registered trademark of Gosling's Export Limited; Häagen-Dazs registered trademark is licensed to Nestlé by General Mills; Hamburger Helper is a registered trademark of General Mills, Inc.; Heinz is a registered trademark of H.J. Heinz Company; Hellman's is a registered trademark of the Unilever Group of Companies; Igloo is a registered trademark of Igloo Products Corp.; Kellogg's Corn Flakes is a registered trademark of the Kellogg Company; Koeze peanut butter is a registered trademark of Koeze Company; Kraft Grated Parmesan Cheese is a registered trademark of Kraft Foods Global Brands, LLC; Jell-O is a registered trademark of Kraft Foods Global brands, LLC; Jolly Green Giant is a registered trademark of General Mills; La Colombe is a registered trademark of La Colombe Torrefaction, Inc.; La Rossa is a registered trademark of Heineken Italia SpA; Lea & Perrins is a registered trademark of Lea & Perrins, Inc.; Lipton is a registered trademark of the Unilever Group of Companies; McCormick's is a registered trademark of McCormick and Co., Inc.; Niman Ranch is a registered trademark of Niman Ranch, Inc.; Old Bay seasoning is a registered trademark of McCormick and Co., Inc.; Pillsbury is a registered trademark of General Mills, Inc.; Pusser's is a registered trademark of Pussers Rum Ltd.; Rice-A-Roni is a registered trademark of the Quaker Oats Company; Ritz is a registered trademarks of Kraft Foods Global Brands, LLC.; Sara Lee is a registered trademark of Sara Lee TM Holdings LLC; Shiner Bock is a registered trademark of Spoetzl Brewery, Inc.; Tabasco is a registered trademark of the McIlhenny Co.; Top Chef is a registered trademark of Bravo Media LLC.; Weber is a registered trademark of Weber-Stephen Products LLC.; Whole Foods is a registered trademark of Whole Foods Market LP, IP; Wray & Nephew is a registered trademark of J. Wray & Nephew Company.